T0345653

Praise for *Software Requirements Essentials*

"As research for a book, I once read the ten best-selling requirements engineering books of the prior ten years. This one book succinctly presents more useful information than those ten books combined. I wish I'd had it as a reference then."

—*Mike Cohn, author of* User Stories Applied *and co-founder of the Scrum Alliance*

"Diamonds come about when a huge amount of carbon atoms are compressed. The compression crystallizes to form diamonds. Karl and Candase have done something very similar: they have compressed their vast requirements knowledge into 20 gems they call 'core practices.'

"These 20 practices give you the essence of requirements discovery, and for extra convenience they are categorized to make your requirements journey more effective. These practices are potent stuff, and I recommend that they become part of everyone's requirements arsenal."

—*James Robertson, author of* Mastering the Requirements Process *and* Business Analysis Agility

"What a valuable resource for new and experienced business analysts alike, who want an accessible, clearly written, and well-organized introduction to key business analyst practices. Karl and Candase do a great job of breaking down a complex role into a straightforward set of practices that can be integrated into your business analysis process to make it more effective."

—*Laura Brandenburg, author of* How to Start a Business Analyst Career

"Candase and Karl have drawn upon their deep knowledge and experience of what it takes to elicit, identify, represent, communicate, and validate requirements for software products effectively. They have produced a useful, accessible, and clear book, which is full of practical advice, great examples, and answers to the hard questions that people building software products face in the real world. If you're involved in building software in any role, this book will give you guidance on ways to make sure the product meets customer needs and delivers real value."

—*Shane Hastie, Global Delivery Lead at SoftEd and Lead Editor, Culture and Methods at InfoQ.com*

"*Software Requirements Essentials* will be a high-value addition to your business analysis library. I give the book high marks, as it does an excellent job of selecting and comprehensively covering the most essential business analysis practices teams should be considering. I thoroughly appreciated that the content was not overdone. Lessons were succinct while remaining extremely usable. Care was taken to ensure the guidance was applicable whether you are using a waterfall, agile, or hybrid delivery approach. I believe anyone looking to improve their business analysis practices will find great practical advice they'll be able to apply immediately."

—*Laura Paton, Principal Consultant, BA Academy, Inc.*

"Here is a book that all business analysts should have on their shelves, a readable reference that pulls together all the best practices we've been applying in business analysis for 50 years or so. While the book is aimed at the experienced BA, Karl and Candase thoughtfully provide an opening chapter reviewing the basic precepts and principles of business analysis. The book is written in Karl's inimitable easy-to-read style, so even beginning BAs can understand and apply the practices. Karl and Candase have made the book 'agile' with lots of practices applicable both to the traditional BA approach and to the BA who's defining user stories for the agile software developers.

"*Software Requirements Essentials* encapsulates all of the excellent advice and counsel Karl has given us over the years into this one touchstone of a book. I wish that I had written it."

—*Steve Blais, author of* Business Analysis: Best Practices for Success *and co-author of* Business Analysis for Practitioners

"One of the many aspects of Karl Wiegers's latest book that we love is the universality of the requirements techniques he describes. Using real-life examples and easy-to-understand illustrations, Wiegers and Candase Hokanson describe practices that can be applied regardless of the project at hand or the methodology followed. They emphasize that there is no one right way to elicit and manage requirements; rather, they present many tried-and-true practices that lead to successful outcomes. Also helpful are the dozens of questions that business analysts can use to elicit various types of requirements.

"The authors emphasize concepts over methodology-specific terminology to ensure that the practices can be understood and applied as methodologies change. The recurrent themes they mention are spot-on and apply to any development effort. *Software Requirements Essentials* is a must-read for every business analyst who wants to avoid the pitfall of achieving 'project success but product failure.'"

—*Elizabeth Larson and Richard Larson, past co-owners of Watermark Learning and authors of* CBAP Certification Study Guide

"So many product development projects face challenges because the stated requirements are ill-defined. This issue can be addressed by business analysts, or anyone conducting business analysis, if they possess the necessary toolkit of techniques and skills. *Software Requirements Essentials* offers an excellent introduction to the requirements engineering framework, and the techniques it encompasses, in an accessible and engaging way. The book offers invaluable guidance and insights via 20 best practices that are highly relevant, if not essential, for anyone working to define requirements. All business analysts need a mental map of the requirements definition service; this book provides it and more."

—*Dr. Debra Paul, Managing Director, Assist Knowledge Development*

Software Requirements Essentials

Software Requirements Essentials

Core Practices for Successful Business Analysis

Karl Wiegers
Candase Hokanson

♠Addison-Wesley

Boston • Columbus • New York • San Francisco • Amsterdam • Cape Town
Dubai • London • Madrid • Milan • Munich • Paris • Montreal • Toronto • Delhi • Mexico City
São Paulo • Sydney • Hong Kong • Seoul • Singapore • Taipei • Tokyo

Cover image: dani3315/Shutterstock

Many of the designations used by manufacturers and sellers to distinguish their products are claimed as trademarks. Where those designations appear in this book, and the publisher was aware of a trademark claim, the designations have been printed with initial capital letters or in all capitals.

The authors and publisher have taken care in the preparation of this book, but make no expressed or implied warranty of any kind and assume no responsibility for errors or omissions. No liability is assumed for incidental or consequential damages in connection with or arising out of the use of the information or programs contained herein.

For information about buying this title in bulk quantities, or for special sales opportunities (which may include electronic versions; custom cover designs; and content particular to your business, training goals, marketing focus, or branding interests), please contact our corporate sales department at corpsales@pearsoned.com or (800) 382-3419.

For government sales inquiries, please contact governmentsales@pearsoned.com.

For questions about sales outside the U.S., please contact intlcs@pearson.com.

Visit us on the Web: informit.com/aw

Library of Congress Control Number: 2023931578

Copyright © 2023 Karl Wiegers and Seilevel Partners, LP

All rights reserved. This publication is protected by copyright, and permission must be obtained from the publisher prior to any prohibited reproduction, storage in a retrieval system, or transmission in any form or by any means, electronic, mechanical, photocopying, recording, or likewise. For information regarding permissions, request forms and the appropriate contacts within the Pearson Education Global Rights & Permissions Department, please visit www.pearson.com/permissions/.

Printed by Ashford Colour Press Ltd

ISBN-13: 978-0-13-819028-6
ISBN-10: 0-13-819028-3

ScoutAutomatedPrintCode

Pearson's Commitment to Diversity, Equity, and Inclusion

Pearson is dedicated to creating bias-free content that reflects the diversity of all learners. We embrace the many dimensions of diversity, including but not limited to race, ethnicity, gender, socioeconomic status, ability, age, sexual orientation, and religious or political beliefs.

Education is a powerful force for equity and change in our world. It has the potential to deliver opportunities that improve lives and enable economic mobility. As we work with authors to create content for every product and service, we acknowledge our responsibility to demonstrate inclusivity and incorporate diverse scholarship so that everyone can achieve their potential through learning. As the world's leading learning company, we have a duty to help drive change and live up to our purpose to help more people create a better life for themselves and to create a better world.

Our ambition is to purposefully contribute to a world where:

- Everyone has an equitable and lifelong opportunity to succeed through learning.
- Our educational products and services are inclusive and represent the rich diversity of learners.
- Our educational content accurately reflects the histories and experiences of the learners we serve.
- Our educational content prompts deeper discussions with learners and motivates them to expand their own learning (and worldview).

While we work hard to present unbiased content, we want to hear from you about any concerns or needs with this Pearson product so that we can investigate and address them.

- Please contact us with concerns about any potential bias at https://www.pearson.com/report-bias.html.

For Chris, naturally
　　　　　　　—K.W.

For Peter and Edward
　　　　　　　—C.H.

Contents

Foreword xvii

Acknowledgments xix

About the Authors xxi

Chapter 1: Essentials of Software Requirements 1

   Requirements Defined 2

   Good Practices for Requirements Engineering 5

   Who Does All This Stuff? 8

   Some Recurrent Themes 9

   The Life and Times of Requirements 11

   Getting Started 11

Chapter 2: Laying the Foundation 13

   Practice #1: Understand the problem before converging on
      a solution 14

      Business Problems 14

      Eliciting the Real Problems 15

      Keeping the Business Problem in Focus 17

      Related Practices 18

      Next Steps 18

   Practice #2: Define business objectives. 19

      Business Requirements 19

      Business Objectives 22

      Success Metrics 23

      Product Vision 24

      Related Practices 25

      Next Steps 26

   Practice #3: Define the solution's boundaries. 26

Refining the Solution Concept 27

Setting the Context 28

Expanding the Ecosystem 29

Applying the Solution's Boundaries 30

Related Practices 32

Next Steps 32

Practice #4: Identify and characterize stakeholders 33

The Quest for Stakeholders 34

Stakeholders, Customers, and User Classes 36

Characterizing Stakeholders 37

Related Practices 39

Next Steps 39

Practice #5: Identify empowered decision makers. 39

Who Makes the Call?. 40

How Do They Decide? 41

What Happens Following the Decision? 43

Related Practices 43

Next Steps 44

Chapter 3: Requirements Elicitation. 45

Practice #6: Understand what users need to do with the solution. 47

Focusing on Usage. 47

Eliciting User Requirements 48

Anatomy of a Use Case 51

Applying Usage-centric Requirements Information 52

Related Practices 52

Next Steps 53

Practice #7: Identify events and responses. 53

Types of Events 54

Specifying Events. 55

Related Practices 59

Next Steps 59

Practice #8: Assess data concepts and relationships. 59

Understanding Data Objects and Their Relationships 60

Refining the Data Understanding 62

Data Details Determine Success 64

Find Data Requirements Wherever They Are Hiding 66

Related Practices 67

Next Steps 67

Practice #9: Elicit and evaluate quality attributes. 67

Eliciting Quality Attributes 68

Quality Attribute Implications 69

Quality Attribute Trade-offs 70

Specifying Quality Attributes 71

Related Practices 73

Next Steps 73

Chapter 4: Requirements Analysis **75**

Practice #10: Analyze requirements and requirement sets. 76

Analyzing Individual Requirements 77

Analyzing Sets of Requirements 81

Related Practices 83

Next Steps 83

Practice #11: Create requirements models. 84

Selecting the Right Models 85

Using Models to Refine Understanding. 87

Iterative Modeling. 90

Related Practices 91

Next Steps 91

Practice #12: Create and evaluate prototypes. 91

Reasons to Prototype. 92

How to Prototype 93

The Prototype's Fate 96

Related Practices 97

Next Steps 97

Practice #13: Prioritize the requirements. 97

The Prioritization Challenge. 98

Factors That Influence Priority 99

Prioritization Techniques 100

Pairwise Comparison for Prioritizing Quality Attributes 102

Analytical Prioritization Methods. 103

Related Practices 104

Next Steps 105

Chapter 5: Requirements Specification 107

  Practice #14: Write requirements in consistent ways. 109
    Some Common Requirement Patterns 109
    Levels of Abstraction. 111
    Requirement Attributes. 113
    Nonfunctional Requirements 114
    Related Practices 115
    Next Steps 115
  Practice #15: Organize requirements in a structured fashion. 115
    Requirements Templates 115
    The Software Requirements Specification. 117
    Requirements Management Tools. 119
    Related Practices 120
    Next Steps 121
  Practice #16: Identify and document business rules. 121
    Business Rules Defined 121
    Discovering Business Rules 123
    Documenting Business Rules. 124
    Applying Business Rules 125
    Related Practices 126
    Next Steps 126
  Practice #17: Create a glossary. 127
    Synchronizing Communication. 127
    Related Practices 130
    Next Steps 130

Chapter 6: Requirements Validation 131

  Practice #18: Review and test the requirements. 132
    Requirements Reviews. 132
    Testing the Requirements 134
    Acceptance Criteria. 135
    Testing Analysis Models 136
    Testing Requirements Efficiently. 138
    Pushing Quality to the Front 139
    Related Practices 140
    Next Steps 140

Chapter 7: Requirements Management 141

    Practice #19: Establish and manage requirements baselines........ 142

        Requirements Baseline Defined.......................... 142

        Two Baselining Strategies 143

        Identifying Which Requirements Are Included in a Baseline.... 144

        Getting Agreement on the Baseline 145

        Managing Multiple Baselines and Changes to Them 147

        Related Practices 148

        Next Steps 149

    Practice #20: Manage changes to requirements effectively. 149

        Anticipating Requirement Changes 150

        Defining the Change Control Process 151

        Assessing Changes for Impacts 154

        After a Decision Is Made.............................. 155

        In Search of Less Change.............................. 155

        Related Practices 155

        Next Steps 156

Appendix: Summary of Practices 157

References 159

Index 165

Foreword

Long story short: If you are going to read only one requirements book, this is it. Karl and Candase have created the long-story-short version of how to develop good requirements on a software project.

Let's back up for the long story. If you made it this far, you already appreciate that good requirements are the foundation of any successful software or systems development project. Whether you're a business analyst, product owner, product manager, business stakeholder, or developer, it's well worth investing the time to elicit, analyze, document, and manage requirements to avoid paying for it later—quite literally. Good requirements lead to high-quality software.

Software Requirements Essentials is designed for the busy practitioner (and who isn't?) as a quick read about the most important requirements practices. It applies to projects using either traditional or agile approaches. The terminology and cadence of these practices may vary, but this book does a nice job of simplifying the differences and pointing out the similarities in those approaches. The practices described apply to virtually any kind of team building virtually any kind of product.

I know Karl and Candase very well personally and can attest to the strength of their collaboration. They each have areas of deep knowledge that complement one another, both extending and balancing each other's ideas. They also both live by what they say, having used the techniques themselves on many projects.

When it comes to comprehensive requirements books, I'm slightly biased in that I do love *Software Requirements, Third Edition*, which I coauthored with Karl. What many don't know is that I learned to be a business analyst from the first edition of *Software Requirements*. In fact, that's when I first met Karl. My job in the late 1990s was to define requirements practices for an agile-like iterative development approach at my software company. Boy, do I ever wish I had had this book back then!

Software Requirements Essentials distills the wealth of information found in *Software Requirements* and many other texts down to twenty of the most important requirements activities that apply on nearly all projects. Today's busy BA simply doesn't have the time to read a lengthy instructive guide front to back. But they should find the time to read this book.

This is the CliffsNotes version of many software requirements books, rolled into one. By nature of it being consciously focused and condensed, you should not expect massive details or full examples of every topic in *Software Requirements Essentials*.

For each of the many techniques presented, you'll get a little what, a little why, and a little how—enough to get you started and motivated. When you want more, follow the numerous links provided to reference materials.

As with any book by Karl, there is lots of practicality to it, with a dash of humor. Candase brings a long history of agile experience, keeping the text modern for today's common practices. Together, they've done a fine job of making this book highly relatable by pulling from their collective wealth of project experiences. The many real-life anecdotes make the recommended techniques real and justify their validity.

You don't have to read *Software Requirements Essentials*. But if you deal with requirements in any capacity on a software project, I'd consider it ... a requirement!

—Joy Beatty, COO, ArgonDigital

Acknowledgments

In preparing this book, we had valuable discussions with Jim Brosseau, Mike Cohn, Jennifer Colburn, David Mantica, Ramsay Millar, and Meilir Page-Jones. We thank them sincerely for their time and expert input. James Robertson eloquently reminded us of how important it is to understand the problem rather than assuming a proposed solution is correct. We appreciate Holly Lee Sefton sharing her expertise on data elicitation and governance. Eugenia Schmidt kindly provided an insightful quotation on requirements analysis, and Tim Lister allowed us to share his succinct definition of project success.

We greatly appreciate the helpful manuscript review input provided by Jeremy Beard, Tanya Charbury, Jennifer Colburn, James Compton, Mihai Gherghelescu, Lisa Hill, Fabrício Laguna, Reneé Lasswell, Linda Lewis, Geraldine Mongold, Meilir Page-Jones, Laura Paton, Maud Schlich, Eugenia Schmidt, James Shields, and Tom Tomasovic. Review comments from Joy Beatty, Runna Hammad, and Holly Lee Sefton were especially valuable.

Many thanks to Noor Ghafoor, Joyce Grapes, and Joe Hawes at ArgonDigital, who helped with prototype wireframes, example models, and glossary entries. Early editorial reviews by Erin Miller were particularly helpful.

Special thanks go to Jim Brosseau of Clarrus for his generous permission to include a version of his quality attribute prioritization spreadsheet tool in the supplementary materials for the book.

We're grateful to Haze Humbert, Menka Mehta, and the production team at Pearson Education for their fine editorial and production work on the manuscript. We also thank ArgonDigital and particularly Joy Beatty for their steadfast support for, and many contributions to, this project.

Working with a coauthor brings numerous benefits. It's tremendously helpful to have someone to bounce ideas off, to clarify your thinking, to improve your presentation, and to contribute new content, fresh perspectives, and unique project experiences. Two authors generate a synergy that lets them tell a richer story than either could on their own. Karl thanks Candase for contributing all those benefits, sharing her extensive experience on agile projects, and adding many illuminating true stories to this book.

As always, Karl is indebted to his wife, Chris, for patiently tolerating yet another book project. She's heard way more about software development and book writing over the years than she ever expected or cared to.

Candase is extremely grateful to her family for supporting her in her first book-writing experience. Special thanks go to her project teammates at ArgonDigital and at her major consulting client for their encouragement even during long and arduous product launches. Two people at ArgonDigital stand out for particular thanks: Joy Beatty for her encouragement and guidance in becoming an author and Megan Stowe for always inspiring Candase to continue learning. Finally, Candase would like to thank Karl for giving her the opportunity to coauthor with him, for being a great mentor through the publishing process, and for making the work fun and enjoyable.

About the Authors

Since 1997, Karl Wiegers has been Principal Consultant with Process Impact, a software development consulting and training company in Happy Valley, Oregon. He has delivered more than 650 presentations to thousands of students and conference attendees worldwide. Previously, he spent eighteen years at Kodak, where he held positions as a photographic research scientist, software developer, software manager, and software process and quality improvement leader. Karl received a PhD in organic chemistry from the University of Illinois.

Karl is the author of thirteen previous books, including *Software Requirements, More About Software Requirements, Software Development Pearls, The Thoughtless Design of Everyday Things, Practical Project Initiation, Peer Reviews in Software*, and a forensic mystery novel titled *The Reconstruction*. He has written many articles on software development, management, design, consulting, chemistry, military history, and self-help. Several of Karl's books have won awards, most recently the Society for Technical Communication's Award of Excellence for *Software Requirements, Third Edition* (coauthored with Joy Beatty). Karl has served on the Editorial Board for *IEEE Software* magazine and as a contributing editor for *Software Development* magazine.

When he's not at the keyboard, Karl enjoys wine tasting, volunteering at the public library, delivering Meals on Wheels, wine tasting, playing guitar, writing and recording songs, wine tasting, reading military history, traveling, and wine tasting. You can reach him through www.processimpact.com and www.karlwiegers.com.

Candase Hokanson is a Business Architect and PMI-Agile Certified Practitioner at ArgonDigital, a software development, professional services, and training company based in Austin, Texas. With over ten years of experience in product ownership and business analysis, Candase works with clients to identify and implement the requirements that generate the best return on investment for their projects, regardless of the development life cycle. She has also trained or coached several hundred fellow product owners and business analysts. Her current passions are understanding how to optimize agile in large enterprises and agile requirements for very technical or back-end systems. Candase graduated from Rice University with a BS and an MS in civil engineering and a BA in religious studies.

Candase is an active member of the product management and business analysis communities, previously serving as a co-chair for the Keep Austin Agile conference in 2019 and president of the Austin IIBA. She has authored multiple articles on using visual models in agile, requirements in agile, and agile in the large enterprise.

Outside of work, Candase enjoys spending time with her family, all things Disney related, reading about British history, traveling, and wine tasting. You can reach her through www.argondigital.com and candase.hokanson@argondigital.com.

Chapter 1

Essentials of Software Requirements

Many years ago, I (Karl) would sometimes dive into writing a new program based on nothing more than an initial idea. I'd spend time coding, executing, fixing, and making a mess in my source code editor as I fumbled around, trying to get results. Eventually, I realized that the root of the problem was rushing to code without having an end point in mind—coding's fun! Those frustrating experiences taught me the importance of thinking through some requirements—objectives, usage tasks, data elements, and more—before doing anything else. After I adjusted my process to understand my requirements first, I never again felt like a software project was out of control.

All projects have requirements. Some teams begin with crisply defined business objectives, other teams receive a rich description of the desired solution's capabilities and characteristics, and still others start with only a fuzzy new product concept. Regardless of the starting point, all participants eventually must reach a shared understanding of what the team is supposed to deliver.

Some project participants aren't very interested in requirements. Certain managers may claim they're too busy to engage in requirements discussions. But then their expectations surface after the product has progressed to the point where major changes mean expensive rework. Some technical people might regard the time spent exploring and documenting requirements as a distraction from the real work of crafting code. However, a good set of requirements lets you answer some important—and universal—questions.

- Why are we working on this?
- Who are we trying to satisfy?

- What are we trying to build?
- What functionality do we implement first? Next? Maybe never?
- How can we tell if our solution[1] is good enough?
- How do we know when we're done?

This book describes the twenty most important practices that help software teams create a set of requirements to serve as the foundation for the subsequent development work. These practices broadly apply regardless of the type of product the team is creating or their development approach. Some software teams work not on discrete development projects but on existing products that demand ongoing modifications and new functionality. The people who are responsible for requirements work on product teams like those will find the practices in this book equally applicable to their work.

The requirements terminology differs between traditional (plan-driven or predictive) and agile (change-driven or adaptive) projects. Regardless of the terminology used, developers still need the same information to build the right solution correctly (Wiegers and Beatty, n.d.a). Some teams will perform certain practices iteratively, delivering value in small chunks. Others may do much of the requirements work early in the project because the problem is well understood. A startup that's trying to assess its product's market fit will focus on exploring ideas and approaches rather than trying to assemble a detailed specification. Whichever way you plan your development cycles, performing these twenty practices well can make the difference between delivering a solution that satisfies your stakeholders and creating one that does not.

Requirements Defined

Now that we've used the word *requirement* several times, we should define what we mean. A software team must deal with many types of requirements-related knowledge, and people will be confused if they lack a common understanding of them. Although it's not fully inclusive, one useful definition of *requirement* comes from Ian Sommerville and Pete Sawyer (1997):

> Requirements are ... a specification of what should be implemented. They are descriptions of how the system should behave, or of a system property or attribute. They may be a constraint on the development process of the system.

---

1. A *project* is an initiative that's launched to create a solution for one or more business problems or to exploit a business opportunity. A *solution* involves creating or modifying one or more products, which could include software systems, manual operations, and business processes. This book uses the terms *product*, *system*, and *application* interchangeably to refer to whatever your team is building.

This definition points out that requirements encompass multiple types of information. However, one aspect lacking from that definition is the concept of a requirement as a statement of a stakeholder need, which is the real starting point for all discussions about requirements.

Several classification schemas and models are in common use to describe various kinds of requirements information (Robertson and Robertson 2013, Wiegers and Beatty 2013, IIBA 2015). They generally agree but differ in some terminology details. In this book, we'll use the model shown in Figure 1.1.

This model shows various categories of requirements information (ovals) as well as containers in which to store that information (rectangles). For simplicity, this book will refer to those containers as documents. They could just as well be spreadsheets, databases, requirements management tools, issue tracking tools, wikis, or a wall covered with sticky notes—whatever works for your team. The container itself is less important than the information it holds and how you choose to record, organize, and communicate that information.

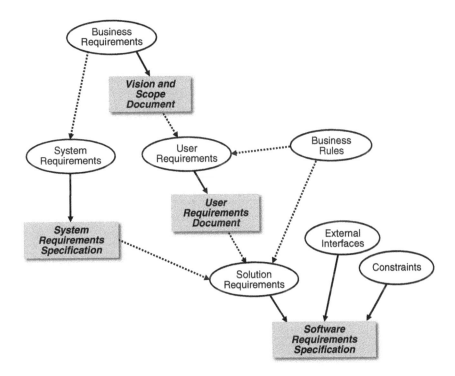

Figure 1.1 *Connections between several types of requirements information and containers that store them. Solid lines mean "are stored in." Dotted lines mean "are the origin of" or "influence."*

Models like that in Figure 1.1 illustrate that there are many types of requirements information. This book uses the definitions in Table 1.1, which are broadly accepted in the requirements engineering and business analysis domains. Note that solution requirements encompass functional, nonfunctional, and data requirements (IIBA 2015). You'll see examples of these various items in later chapters. This book uses the collective term *requirements* to refer to all of these types of information, whether your local terminology focuses on features, use cases, user stories, or anything else.

Table 1.1 *Definitions of several types of requirements information*

Type of information	Definition
Business requirement	Information that describes why the organization is undertaking the project, establishes business objectives, defines a product vision, and includes other direction-setting information. (See Practice #2, "Define business objectives.")
Business rule	A directive that defines or restricts actions within an organization's operations. A policy, regulation, law, or standard that leads to derived solution requirements that enforce or comply with it. (See Practice #16, "Identify and document business rules.")
Constraint	A restriction imposed on the requirements, design, or implementation activities.
Data requirement	A definition of a data object or element that the system must manipulate, its composition and attributes, relationships among data objects, and their input and output formats. (See Practice #8, "Assess data concepts and relationships.")
External interface requirement	A description of a connection between the solution being built and other elements of the world around it, including users, other software systems, hardware devices, and networks.
Functional requirement	A description of some behavior that the product will exhibit under specified circumstances.
Nonfunctional requirement	Most commonly refers to what is also known as a *quality attribute* requirement. Quality attributes describe various quality, service, or performance characteristics of the solution. (See Practice #9, "Elicit and evaluate quality attributes.")
Solution requirement	A description of a capability or characteristic that the product being created must possess to satisfy certain user requirements and help achieve the project's business objectives. Solution requirements include functional, nonfunctional, and data requirements, as well as manual operations.
System requirement	A description of a top-level capability or characteristic of a complex system that has multiple subsystems, often including both hardware and software elements. System requirements serve as the origin of derived software solution requirements.

Table 1.1 (continued)

Type of information	Definition
User requirement	A description of a task or goal that a user wishes to accomplish with the solution. The International Institute of Business Analysis generalizes this category to "stakeholder requirements," but in actuality, all requirements originate from some stakeholder (IIBA 2015). Here, we're specifically referring to things the *user* needs to do and user-specific expectations the solution must satisfy. (See Practice #6, "Understand what users need to do with the solution.")

The fact that the diagonal arrows in Figure 1.1 that lead from Business Requirements down to the Software Requirements Specification are all aligned is no accident. Developers do not directly implement business requirements or user requirements. They implement functional requirements, including those derived from other categories of requirements information. The goal is to implement the right set of functionality that lets users perform their tasks and satisfies their quality expectations, thereby (hopefully) achieving the project's business requirements, within all imposed constraints. That "right set" of functional requirements comes from a foundation of well-understood business and user requirements.

Not every requirement will fit tidily into one or another of the categories in Table 1.1. Debating exactly what to call a specific statement is not important. What's important is that the team recognizes the need, analyzes it, records it in an appropriate form and location, and builds whatever is necessary to satisfy it.

Good Practices for Requirements Engineering

The domain of requirements engineering is broadly divided into *requirements development* and *requirements management*. Requirements development encompasses the activities a team performs to identify, understand, and communicate requirements knowledge. Requirements management deals with taking care of requirements once you have them in hand. Requirements management activities include handling the inevitable changes, tracking versions of requirements and their status over time, and tracing individual requirements to related requirements, design components, code, tests, and other elements.

Requirements development is further partitioned into four subdomains:

Elicitation	Activities to collect, discover, and invent requirements. Sometimes called gathering requirements, but elicitation is much more than a collection process.
Analysis	Activities to assess requirements for their details, value, interconnections, feasibility, and other properties to reach a

sufficiently precise understanding to implement the requirements at low risk.

Specification   Activities to represent requirements knowledge in appropriate and persistent forms so that they can be communicated to
others.

Validation   Activities to assess the extent to which requirements will
satisfy a stakeholder need.

These four sets of activities are not simply performed in a linear, one-pass
sequence. As Figure 1.2 illustrates, they are interwoven and repeated until a particular set of requirements is understood well enough that the development team can
build and verify that part of the solution with confidence. Requirements development is an incremental and iterative process by necessity, frustrating though that can
be for the participants. Exploring requirements is an investment that reduces uncertainty and improves efficiency. The process might feel slow, but requirements thinking saves time in the end.

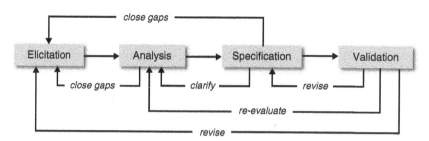

Figure 1.2 *Requirements elicitation, analysis, specification, and validation are performed
incrementally, iteratively, and often concurrently.*

Each of the requirements engineering subdomains encompasses numerous discrete practices. That's what this book is about. It describes twenty core practices that
are particularly strong contributors to success on nearly all projects. Whether you
lead requirement efforts, take part in them, or depend on them to perform your own
work, you'll be more effective if you apply these core practices. Several of the practices refer to templates, spreadsheet tools, checklists, and other work aids, which you
may download from the website associated with this book at www.informit.com.

We've grouped the practices by requirements engineering subdomain, four
for requirements development and one for requirements management. Chapter 3
addresses requirements elicitation, Chapter 4 describes analysis practices, Chapter 5
deals with requirements specification, and Chapter 6 discusses key validation practices. The most important requirements management practices appear in Chapter 7.

Each practice description presents numerous practical techniques, identifies related practices, and suggests several Next Steps to help you put the practice into action right away. The practice descriptions are relatively short, so we've provided many references to other sources where you can get more detailed information.

Some practices in the elicitation chapter also describe related analysis and specification activities for topics like quality attributes and data. This grouping underscores the intrinsic entanglement of these requirements subdomains. It's not a clean separation.

You might have noticed that we skipped past Chapter 2. That chapter discusses five additional requirements-related activities that every project should perform to lay a solid foundation for a successful outcome. You're well served to conduct those activities early on to align all the stakeholders toward common goals, rather than going back to address them later when the team runs into problems.

This set of practices does not constitute a one-size-fits-all requirements process. When developing software, whoever leads the requirements work should work with other leaders to decide which requirements approaches will be most effective. Factors to consider include the project's nature and size, the team's experience with similar products, the access the team will have to stakeholders, particular areas of requirements risk, constraints, and organizational cultures (IIBA 2015). Select those practices that you believe will add the most value to the work, and adapt the practice descriptions from this book and other sources to best meet your specific needs.

The Appendix lists all twenty practices we address. These are by no means the only available requirements techniques. Numerous comprehensive (meaning long) books describe dozens of practices for requirements engineering and business analysis. These are some of the most useful resources:

- *Software Requirements, 3rd Edition* by Karl Wiegers and Joy Beatty (Microsoft Press, 2013)

- *Mastering the Requirements Process: Getting Requirements Right, 3rd Edition* by Suzanne Robertson and James Robertson (Addison-Wesley, 2013)

- *Agile Software Requirements: Lean Requirements Practices for Teams, Programs, and the Enterprise* by Dean Leffingwell (Addison-Wesley, 2011)

- *Business Analysis: Best Practices for Success* by Steven P. Blais (John Wiley & Sons, Inc., 2012)

- *Business Analysis, 4th Edition* by Debra Paul and James Cadle (BCS, The Chartered Institute for IT, 2020)

- *A Guide to the Business Analysis Body of Knowledge (BABOK Guide), 3rd Edition* (International Institute of Business Analysis, 2015)

- *Business Analysis for Practitioners: A Practice Guide* (Project Management Institute, Inc., 2015)

- *The PMI Guide to Business Analysis* (Project Management Institute, Inc., 2017)

We encourage you to refer to books like those for more information on the topics we discuss here, as well as to learn about other practices you might find helpful. A professional in the requirements field must accumulate a rich tool kit of practices and techniques, along with the experience to know which tool is the best one to use in each situation.

Some books or development frameworks recommend that you discard certain established practices and replace them with others. That's poor advice. You should *add* new practices to your tool kit, discarding older ones only when you can replace them with something that's demonstrably better in all situations. If something works for you, why throw it away?

Who Does All This Stuff?

Historically, someone responsible for developing and managing requirements on a software project was called a *requirements analyst*, *systems analyst*, *business systems analyst*, or simply *analyst*. Large projects, particularly those building systems with both hardware and software components, might have *requirements engineers* who perform this function. Organizations that create commercial software products use *product managers* to bridge the gap between marketing and the development team. Agile development teams often include a *product owner* who defines and manages the requirements and other work items—collectively called product backlog items— that will lead to the solution.

In recent years, the term *business analyst* has largely replaced those historical job titles. This book uses *business analyst*, or BA, to refer to whomever on a development team has responsibility for requirements. In many organizations, a BA's role extends beyond dealing with requirements, but we will focus on their requirements activities.

Note that *business analyst* refers to a role, not necessarily a job title. Even if the team lacks an official BA, someone still must elicit, analyze, specify, validate, and manage its requirements. This work could be divided among multiple individuals, possibly including a project manager, quality assurance leader, and developers. When a team member who has another title is performing this kind of work, they are acting as a BA.

Because the requirements domain is both critical and complex, it's unrealistic to expect any random team member to perform the BA role without some education about how to do it well. A capable BA brings a particular set of knowledge, experience, personality characteristics, and skills to the process, including those listed in Table 1.2 (Wiegers and Beatty 2013). If you're working in this role, assess your capabilities in each category and then work to improve those that aren't as strong as others.

Table 1.2 *Some valuable business analyst skills and characteristics*

Listening	Writing
Interviewing and questioning	Modeling
Facilitation	Flexibility across the abstraction scale
Nonverbal communication	Organizing information and activities
Analytical thinking	Handling interpersonal interactions
Systems thinking	Leadership
Quick thinking	Creativity
Observation	Curiosity

In recent years, several organizations have recognized the great value that business analysts and requirements engineers can contribute. These organizations have developed bodies of knowledge and professional certifications that people working in these fields can pursue. Such professional organizations include

- The International Institute of Business Analysis (IIBA), iiba.org
- The International Requirements Engineering Board (IREB), ireb.org
- The Project Management Institute (PMI), pmi.org

The bodies of knowledge these organizations have accumulated are rich sources of information about the many requirements processes, techniques, and tools that contribute to success.

Some Recurrent Themes

Some common themes run through this book. Keep the following themes in mind as you select practices to use on your projects and tailor them to suit each situation.

- **Requirements development demands an incremental and iterative approach.** It's highly unlikely that anyone will think of all the requirements before development begins and that they will remain unchanged. People get more information, have fresh ideas, remember things they had overlooked, change their minds, and must adapt to changing business and technical realities.

- No matter how you choose to represent requirements knowledge, **the goal of all specification activities is clear and effective communication.** The artifacts the BA produces have multiple audiences. Those audiences may wish to see information presented in different forms and at various levels of detail. Consider those diverse audiences as you create requirements deliverables.

- **Requirements engineering is a collaborative process.** Requirements affect all stakeholders. Many people can supply input to the requirements, many people do work based on them, and many people use the resultant solution. Customer engagement is a powerful contributor to a successful outcome. The BA must work with people who can accurately present the needs of diverse stakeholder communities. Most requirements decisions involve multiple participants with different, and sometimes conflicting, interests and priorities.

- **Change happens.** A solution-development effort is chasing a moving target. Business needs, technologies, markets, regulations, and users change. A BA must keep up with evolving needs and make sure that changes are clearly understood, recorded, and communicated to those they affect.

- A powerful way to increase development productivity is to minimize the amount of rework the team must perform. Therefore, try to **push quality activities to the front** of the development cycle—that is, earlier rather than later. Better requirements pay off with less rework later in development or following delivery.

- **Use risk thinking** to decide which requirements practices to employ, when to perform them, when to stop, and how much detail is necessary. For instance, the risks of miscommunication and wasted effort are greater when development is outsourced or teams are remote than when participants work in proximity. Therefore, requirements for such projects must be written more precisely and in more detail than when developers can quickly get answers from the people around them.

The Life and Times of Requirements

Neither requirements development nor requirements management activities end when the initial project team delivers the solution. They continue throughout the product's operational or market life, as it evolves through an ongoing series of enhancement and maintenance cycles. As change requests arrive, someone must elicit the corresponding requirements details and evaluate their impact on the current solution. They must then document the new or changed requirements, validate them, track their implementation status, trace them to other system elements, and so forth.

The BA should look for existing requirements-related items from other projects they could reuse. At times, they might create deliverables that have reuse potential elsewhere in the organization. Glossaries, business rules, process descriptions, stakeholder catalogs, data models, security requirements, and the like can apply to multiple situations. Once an organization invests in creating these artifacts, it should organize them to enable reuse and look for opportunities to leverage that investment further (Wiegers and Beatty 2013).

Getting Started

This book contains a lot of information and recommends many practices and techniques. Some of these you no doubt already perform; others might be new to you. We have two pieces of advice about getting started with the practices we suggest.

1. Don't feel bad if you don't already perform all these activities on your projects.

2. Don't try to do everything at once.

As you read, identify those practices that you think would add the most value to your project. Look for opportunities to try them and situations in which they might yield better results. Recognize the reality that the learning curve will slow you down a bit as you try to figure out how to make new methods work for you and your colleagues. Follow the references we've provided to learn more about those practices that look interesting to you. Over time, new ways of working will become part of your BA tool kit—and you will get better results.

Whether you call it business analysis or requirements engineering, it's a challenging, yet vital, function. The core practices described in this book give you solid tools to tackle this critical activity with confidence.

Chapter 2

Laying the Foundation

In the classical pure (and hypothetical) waterfall software development model, the team accumulates a complete set of requirements for the product, designs a solution, builds the entire solution, tests it all, and delivers it. We all know that approach doesn't work well in most cases.

Projects will vary in how much requirements work can, and should, be done up front. Sometimes it's possible to specify a good portion of the requirements for an information system before getting too far into implementation. Complex products with multiple hardware and software components demand careful requirements engineering because the cost of making late changes is high. For applications that change rapidly or lend themselves to incrementally releasing ever more capable software versions, developing requirements just-in-time in small chunks is an effective approach. Innovative apps may involve a lot of concept exploration, prototyping, feasibility studies, and market assessment.

No single approach to the development life cycle or requirements work optimally fits every situation. However, there are several interconnected activities related to requirements that every team should perform at the beginning. This chapter describes five essential practices that collectively provide a solid foundation for both technical and business success:

Practice #1. Understand the problem before converging on a solution.

Practice #2. Define business objectives.

Practice #3. Define the solution's boundaries.

Practice #4. Identify and characterize stakeholders.

Practice #5. Identify empowered decision makers.

Practice #1	Understand the problem before converging on a solution.

Imagine that you worked for more than a year on a project that had executive support and high visibility. In your business analyst role, you performed the requirements elicitation, analysis, and specification. The development team built what the stakeholders asked for and deployed the product on schedule. But just three months later, the product is considered a failure and decommissioned. Why? Because it didn't solve the right problem.

Far too often, teams build and release requirements, features, and even entire products that go unused because those teams didn't fully understand the business situation and the problems they were trying to solve. Understanding the problems or opportunities that your solution will address aligns all participants on the core issues and provides confidence that the solution will indeed achieve the desired outcomes.

Business Problems

A business problem is any issue that prevents the business from achieving its goals or exploiting an opportunity (Beatty and Chen 2012). A business problem can be small, such as a user complaint that some task takes too long, which can perhaps be solved by streamlining some functionality. Or it can be as large as organization-level business challenges—spending too much money, not making enough money, or losing money—that demand major projects or entirely new products.

Organizations launch initiatives to solve one or more business problems. Each activity gets funded because management expects its business value to outweigh its costs. However, those problems or opportunities often are neither explicitly stated nor documented. Rather than presenting a clear problem statement, the executive sponsor or lead customer might simply tell the team what to build. This can cause the scenario described above: project success but product failure. If you don't understand the problem adequately, or if you begin with a specific solution in mind, there's a good chance that the team will solve only part of the problem—or perhaps none of it.

It's a good idea to avoid presuming that either a presented problem or a presented solution is necessarily correct. That initial presentation might come from a business case, project charter, senior manager, or product visionary. But can you trust it as setting the right direction for all the work that will follow?

When you're presented with a stated problem, perform a *root cause analysis* until you're confident that the real issue and its contributing factors are well understood (Tableau 2022). Then you can derive possible solutions that you know will address those very issues. If you're presented with a solution, explore this question: "If <*solution*> is the answer, what was the question?" In other words, ask "Why do you think that's the right solution?" You might discover that the underlying issue demands a different approach: possibly simpler, possibly more complex, possibly more specific, possibly more general. You won't know until you perform the analysis.

Eliciting the Real Problems

A stakeholder might request a solution such as "Combine several systems into one," with the expectation that such a strategy would address multiple, unspecified objectives. However, system consolidation could be overkill if a simpler answer is appropriate. If the problem is that you're spending too much money on maintenance and support for four existing systems, combining them could be the right approach. However, suppose that the most pressing concern instead is that your users are unhappy. A root cause analysis using the 5 *Whys* technique with the pertinent stakeholders could sort all this out (Tableau 2022).

Root cause analysis involves working backward from a stated problem or a proposed solution to identify the underlying problems and the factors that contribute to them. Assessing those factors then leads to the appropriate solution choice. With the 5 Whys technique, you ask questions like "Why is that a problem?" or "Why are we not already achieving that goal today?" repeatedly until you unveil the compelling issue that drove launching the initiative in the first place. The conversation between a business analyst and a key stakeholder might go something like this:

Analyst: "You requested that we combine your four current systems into one. Why do we need to combine them?"

Stakeholder: "Because our customers complain that they must keep signing in between webpage clicks. It's annoying. This is because they're accessing different backend systems that all have separate user accounts."

Analyst: "Why is it an issue if your customers are complaining?"

Stakeholder: "According to our market research, 25 percent of our customers have left us for the competition because of their frustrations with usability on our site."

Analyst: "If that's the case, why not just implement single sign-on to improve usability?"

Stakeholder: "That would help, but we'd still have to maintain and support all four systems."

Analyst: "If we combined them, wouldn't you still need the same number of support people for the new system?"

Stakeholder: "We don't believe so. The four current systems use different programming languages. We need at least one engineer fluent in each language to support each system, although there's not enough work to keep them busy. By combining the systems into one using a single language, we could free up the additional engineers to work on other products."

Analyst: "Ah, so it looks like you're trying to solve multiple problems. You want higher customer retention, and you also want to reduce support costs and free up staff by using fewer technologies."

By asking "why" several times in this conversation, the analyst now understands that the stakeholder expects their proposed solution to address two significant concerns. The request to combine several systems into one might indeed be the best long-term strategy. However, an interim solution using single sign-on could appease the disgruntled customers quickly, while the consolidation initiative works on the larger concern of support and maintenance.

A root cause analysis diagram, also called a fishbone or Ishikawa diagram, is a way to show the analysis results. Suppose the BA drills down into the first problem the stakeholder brought up: losing frustrated customers. The BA could apply the 5 Whys technique to determine exactly why the customers are frustrated and then draw a diagram like the one in Figure 2.1. The problem goes at the head of the "fish." Place the highest-level causes in the boxes on diagonal lines coming off the fish's backbone. Add contributing causes on the short horizontal lines from each diagonal. Continue the exploration until you reach the ultimate, actionable root causes. Then you can devise one or more solutions to address them.

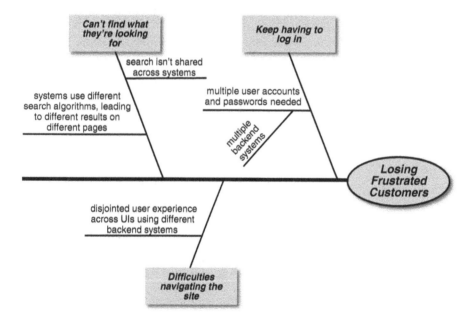

Figure 2.1 *A root cause analysis (fishbone or Ishikawa) diagram example shows the factors that contribute to the stated problem.*

Once you've identified the primary and contributing issues, consider all their implications before committing to a solution. The requested or most apparent solution could be the wrong strategy. On one of Candase's projects, the problem was that the version of the commercial off-the-shelf (COTS) package the company used was going end-of-life soon and the vendor would no longer support it. After that, any production issue could have cost the company its entire business because it wouldn't have any vendor assistance. Nor could it currently make its own enhancements to the vendor product. The obvious solution was to upgrade to the latest version of the vendor's product. However, the company would have had to pay the vendor high service fees to resolve problems and add enhancements. Consequently, the company considered both acquiring a new COTS package from a different vendor and building an in-house replacement as better solutions to both the initial end-of-life concern and the additional issues.

Problem analysis can reveal other, unobvious challenges. You might confront conflicting problems from different stakeholders or be trying to solve multiple, disparate problems with a single fix. As you explore the issues, look for situations where you might need several solutions, rather than seeking a single silver bullet.

Keeping the Business Problem in Focus

When the key stakeholders have agreed upon a clear understanding of the core business concerns, consider writing a problem statement (Kyne 2022). A template like this can be helpful (Compton 2022):

Situation	Describe the background, context, and environment.
Problem	Describe the business problems or opportunities as you now understand them.
Implication	Describe the likely results if the problem isn't solved.
Benefit	State the business value of solving the problem.
Vision	Describe what the desired future state would look like.

A concise problem statement serves as the reference point for the rest of the work. It feeds directly into crafting the specific business objectives that management or your customers expect the solution to achieve (see Practice #2, "Define business objectives"). The problem statement also helps the team make decisions throughout the project. When prioritizing requirements, favor those items that are the most critical or timely contributors to solving the highest-value problem (see Practice #13, "Prioritize the requirements"). In the combine-several-systems-into-one example above, implementing single sign-on to relieve customer frustration would be a quicker fix than combining multiple systems and would address the immediate concern of losing customers.

Whenever someone requests a new system capability, ask how it relates to the business problems (see Practice #20, "Manage changes to requirements effectively"). If you can't tie each new requirement to any of the defined business problems, either there are more problems yet to explore or you don't need the new requirement.

Stakeholders often will propose a specific deliverable as a requirement: "Build me product X or feature Y." The stakeholder's solution may indeed be the correct one—but not necessarily. Take the time to thoroughly understand the real business problem to ensure that the team focuses on achieving the proper outcomes. If your analysis reveals that the real problem doesn't quite match what you found in a business case or other originating document, revise that document to match the newly understood reality. That insight could profoundly change the project's direction.

Related Practices

Practice #2. Define business objectives.

Practice #3. Define the solution's boundaries.

Practice #13. Prioritize the requirements.

Practice #20. Manage changes to requirements effectively.

Next Steps

1. If you haven't already done so, talk with project leadership and key stakeholders about why they're undertaking your initiative to make sure you understand the problem it is intended to solve.

2. Create a root cause analysis diagram for your core business problem, using a technique like 5 Whys to discover both major and contributing causes.

3. Write a problem statement using the template described in this section.

4. Based on the problem or problems identified, assess whether your current solution concept will address them adequately. If not, either change the solution or point out the risk that the current solution may not be sufficient.

| Practice #2 | Define business objectives. |

Understanding the business problems and opportunities is an essential first step in making sure the team focuses on the right concerns. The next step is to describe exactly what the project sponsor or other important stakeholders expect the solution to accomplish. If someone asks why your team is working on a particular initiative, you should have a good answer.

Some people use the term *business requirement* to refer to any requirement, including bits of requested functionality, that comes from the business, but that's not how we use the term. We're referring to information that explains why the organization has decided to undertake the project and what value they expect it to deliver (Wiegers and Beatty 2013). Core elements of the business requirements include statements of business opportunities and objectives, success metrics, and a vision statement. Articulating the business requirements is an essential step in achieving alignment among all stakeholders to create the right solution.

Business Requirements

An organization undertakes an initiative to create or exploit a business opportunity, satisfy a business need, or solve a business problem. Clearly stated business requirements build on the problem statement to specify the desired business outcomes, identify indicators that will tell us when the problem is solved, and much more. Business requirements appear at the top of the requirements model in Figure 1.1. They provide the guiding directives for all the work that follows. If a project or product fails to satisfy its business requirements, someone wasted a lot of time, money, and effort.

Business requirements could originate from an executive who understands the problem, a primary customer who recognizes a need, or a product visionary who sees a market opportunity. Such people might already have established a business case for the initiative, but they still might find it valuable to work with a BA to craft a richer set of business requirements.

If you find yourself facilitating a discussion to explore a project's business drivers and justification, remember that the goal at that stage is not to accumulate an extensive list of desired functionality. Instead, business requirements focus on *why* launching this project or building that product is a good idea. The following questions can stimulate a discussion that yields the relevant information (Business Analysis

Excellence, n.d., Wiegers 2006). The website for this book offers a download with these questions, and others, in the form of checklists.

- What business problem are you trying to solve or what business opportunity do you perceive?

- What's the motivation for solving this problem or pursuing this opportunity, or what points of pain do you hope to relieve?

- What are your business objectives? Why aren't you already achieving those desired outcomes?

- How would the proposed product provide value to the organization, the company, your customers, or humanity as a whole?

- What would a highly successful solution do for you? Can you quantify its potential payoff?

- How could you judge the solution's success?

- What could the business impact be if you *don't* pursue this solution?

- Which individuals, groups, products, systems, or projects could influence or be affected by this project?

- What are the timing goals or constraints for delivering a partial solution? A complete solution?

- If the organization unsuccessfully tried to solve this problem previously, why did the attempt fail and what should the team do differently this time?

- What assumptions are you making regarding the proposed initiative? What risks do you see associated with it?

Business requirements encompass several kinds of information. Many software teams create a vision and scope document that contains the business requirements using a template similar to the one shown in Figure 2.2 (Wiegers and Beatty 2013). Other teams might store that information in a project charter, using a template like the one in Figure 2.3 (Wiegers 2007). Both templates, with embedded guidance text, are available for downloading from the website that accompanies this book. The answers to the questions above let you populate various sections of these templates.

```
1. Business Requirements
   1.1  Background
   1.2  Business Problem or Opportunity
   1.3  Business Objectives
   1.4  Success Metrics
   1.5  Vision Statement
   1.6  Business Risks
   1.7  Business Assumptions and Dependencies
2. Scope and Limitations
   2.1  Major Features
   2.2  Scope of Initial Release
   2.3  Scope of Subsequent Releases
   2.4  Limitations and Exclusions
3. Business Context
   3.1  Stakeholder Profiles
   3.2  Project Priorities
   3.3  Deployment Considerations
```

Figure 2.2 *Suggested template for a vision and scope document (adapted from* Software Requirements, 3rd Edition, *by Karl Wiegers and Joy Beatty).*

```
 1.  Project Description
 2.  Business Objectives and Success Criteria
 3.  Stakeholders
 4.  Vision
 5.  Project Scope
 6.  Assumptions and Dependencies
 7.  Constraints
 8.  Milestones
 9.  Business Risks
10.  Resources
11.  Approvals
```

Figure 2.3 *Suggested template for a project charter (from* Practical Project Initiation *by Karl E. Wiegers).*

Organizations that create commercial software products often write market requirements documents that could include this business information. And any organization could write a business case to justify investing in a new initiative. As business analysis author Steven Blais (2012) points out:

> All of these documents serve the same purpose: to provide the information necessary for someone to make a decision to solve this business problem now, later, or never. The overall goal of the business case is to minimize risk in decision-making.

Business Objectives

Business objectives let you determine when a business problem is solved, a need is fulfilled, or an opportunity is exploited. Business objectives can be financial or non-financial, internal (operations) or outward facing (products), strategic or tactical. While it's easier to state vague goals, you should write your objectives to be specific, realistic, and measurable. Otherwise, you can't tell if you've achieved them.

Setting targets in the form of business objectives lets the decision makers define the scope of work needed to achieve them. The objectives help ensure that the solution includes all the necessary functionality while avoiding extraneous features that don't contribute to the desired business outcomes.

Defining the business objectives up front drives the creation of the solution concept. That concept then leads to activities to define the solution's specific features and attributes, a process called requirements elicitation. Suppose you have a great idea for an innovative new product. You're eager to dive into construction, maybe starting with a proof-of-concept prototype. That exploration is valuable, but before you begin to build the product for real, take the time to think through why you want to build it and what you hope to accomplish: your business objectives.

The simplest approach is to list the objectives you expect any solution to fulfill:

Grow the digital business from ~$1B to $10B in revenue with a 50 to 75 percent margin by 2030.

Reduce the average time spent on document storage and retrieval from 10 hours to 2 hours per employee per week.

It's better to quantify objectives by stating absolute goals, rather than percentage changes relative to a current starting point (Beatty and Chen 2012). For example, instead of this:

Increase market share in the Australasia region by 20 percent within 6 months.

state something like this:

Achieve a market share of at least 45 percent in the Australasia region by October 1, 2024.

Relative changes are hard to assess if the reference baseline value, dates, or measurement method is not precisely stated and recorded.

A *business objectives model* permits a more thorough analysis for complex problems. This diagram is one of many in RML, the requirements modeling language developed by Joy Beatty and Anthony Chen (2012). The business objectives model visually links business problems to business objectives, their associated success metrics, and the resultant solution concept (ArgonDigital 2022). A concise description of how to create a business objectives model is available from the website associated with this book. Figure 2.4 illustrates a partial business objectives model for a hypothetical restaurant online ordering system designed to supplement taking phone orders. We'll see more about this system as we go along.

Modeling is particularly valuable when you have interwoven business problems and objectives: One problem leads to an objective, which leads to a more detailed problem, which leads to another objective, and so on, as in Figure 2.4. A more sophisticated RML model, called the *objective chain*, ties proposed solution features quantitatively to business objectives (Beatty and Chen 2012). The objective chain helps you analyze which features will add the most value to the business or the solution's users and therefore are likely the most important to implement first.

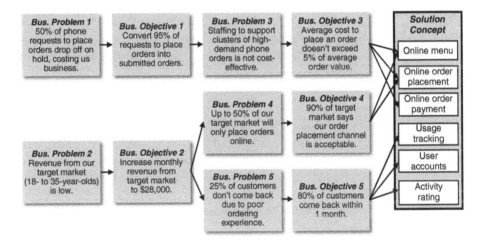

Figure 2.4 *A business objectives model links business problems, business objectives, success metrics, and solution concepts.*

Success Metrics

Success metrics let you judge progress and your solution's contributions toward your objectives. In some cases, the objective lends itself to direct measurement. The business objective stated earlier—"Achieve a market share of at least 45 percent in the Australasia region by October 1, 2024"—is one of those, assuming you can track your market share as a function of time.

However, many business objectives are both lagging indicators (you can't be sure until the end) and potentially influenced by factors beyond your solution. In these situations, you must use metrics that are proxies or surrogates that indicate whether your solution is on track toward achieving the overall business objectives.

If your objective in the year 2023 is to grow revenue to $10B by 2030, you won't know for sure if you've achieved that for seven more years. Even if you do achieve the goal, at least some of the growth could have been due to new marketing or sales activities rather than your product. Interim success metrics, such as the number of new customers or average order size, are indicators that could give you confidence that your solution is doing what you hoped it would. Make sure that trends in the surrogate metrics you select—the tracking indicators—are proportional to what you're really trying to achieve.

Product Vision

A *vision statement*—another component of the business requirements—establishes a high-level, strategic target to align all project participants toward the same outcome. The vision statement succinctly summarizes the ultimate intent for the solution (Wiegers and Beatty 2013). In just a few sentences, the vision statement articulates the essence of the problem, the nature of the proposed solution, its high-level features, and its core benefits for certain stakeholders.

People sometimes lump together vision and scope, but they're different things. We think in terms of a *product* vision—which might never be fully attained—and a *project* scope that defines what portion of the ultimate vision any specific project or development cycle intends to realize. Along with the business objectives, the vision statement describes how some aspect of the world will be better with the new product: who's the target market, what's the product about, why is it better than the current situation, and so on. This simple keyword template is helpful for writing a vision statement (Moore 2014):

For	[target customers]
Who	[statement of the business need or opportunity]
The	[name of the product or project]
Is	[type of product or project]
That	[major product capabilities; core benefits it will provide; compelling reason to buy the product or undertake the project]
Unlike	[current business reality, alternative products, or the competition]
Our product	[concise summary of the major advantages of this product over the current reality or the competition]

The template helps people think through the vision statement elements and write them in a consistent and concise pattern. As an illustration, here's the vision statement we wrote for this book, with the template's keywords highlighted in **bold italics**.

For business analysts, product managers, product owners, requirements engineers, user representatives, developers, testers, and other team members *who* are responsible for requirements development and management activities, ***Software Requirements Essentials is*** a compact book *that* succinctly describes the twenty core requirements practices that all software and systems projects should apply. Each practice is efficiently summarized in a pragmatic style that lets the reader quickly understand why it is important and how to begin applying it.

Unlike the many much longer, comprehensive texts on requirements and business analysis that cover dozens of techniques in hundreds of pages, ***our product*** is a short and highly readable book that focuses on just twenty essential practices in the areas of laying the foundation for a successful project and requirements elicitation, analysis, specification, validation, and management. This brevity and focus increase the appeal to busy practitioners, who can quickly find the useful guidance they need, along with pointers to other sources for further detail.

(As the reader—our customer—you are the ultimate judge of whether we delivered on this vision!)

Creating a vision statement is a collaborative activity, as everyone must be aligned on the product vision. However, rather than asking several stakeholders to concoct a joint vision statement, it's illuminating to have them write their vision statements independently using this template and then compare their results. This exercise can reveal terminology differences, conflicting objectives, emphasis on different user communities, and solution boundary issues that the participants must resolve.

As the team members make countless decisions about their work over time, they should keep the problem statement, business objectives, success metrics, and vision statement in mind. The implemented solution should deliver the value that lets the organization achieve its business objectives. Clearly communicated business requirements set the stage for any information technology project to pay off.

Related Practices

Practice #1. Understand the problem before converging on a solution.

Practice #3. Define the solution's boundaries.

Practice #4. Identify and characterize stakeholders.

Practice #6. Understand what users need to do with the solution.

Next Steps

1. If you don't already have one, invite the key stakeholders who are driving the project to agree upon a vision statement.

2. If your organization doesn't have one yet, propose a template for a business requirements document (or "container") that's tailored to suit the needs and nature of your projects. If you do have a template already, compare it to the content shown in Figures 2.2 and 2.3 and make any appropriate adjustments.

3. Work with the appropriate individuals to craft several quantitative, verifiable business objectives for your project. Confirm that the work underway or planned aligns with achieving those objectives.

4. Define success metrics for each business objective that will reveal whether the solution is moving in the direction of achieving those objectives.

5. If you have multiple interrelated business problems and objectives, draw a business objectives model to show their connections.

Practice #3	Define the solution's boundaries.

When you start a new initiative, you have funding to solve one or more business problems and a high-level concept of a possible solution. However, you might not know exactly where to draw the line between what the solution should and should not include. An important step in laying the foundation for a successful effort is to establish that "what's in, what's out" boundary. You also need to know what changes are needed in the forthcoming solution's environment and where to make them. Questions like these can help you figure all that out.

- Which business processes, functions, and events will be part of the solution? Which ones will remain outside it?

- Who will use or derive benefits from the solution? Who is excluded?

- Which software systems will be part of the solution? What will the interfaces between them look like?

- Where do each system's responsibilities begin and end?

- What data sets, sources, and operations will be incorporated into the solution?

- How do we fit our solution into the rest of our universe?

- How do we know where to stop?

Answering such questions allows the BA to clearly visualize and articulate which software systems, hardware components, and manual operations lie within the chosen solution's scope.

Refining the Solution Concept

To define the solution's boundaries, the BA and the team must refine the intended solution from a mere concept or feature list to a clear statement of what they will build or enhance. Where you position the solution's boundaries will depend on the business objectives and the appetite for—and relative cost of—manual versus automated processes (Robertson and Robertson 2013).

Suppose your project is to implement an online ordering capability for a restaurant. In the current state, the restaurant has only two information systems: a menu repository and an order placement system. A customer gives their order verbally to a restaurant employee either on the phone or in person. The employee then enters the order in the order placement system. The order placement system checks the menu repository to ensure that all items in the order are available. If so, the order placement system generates a ticket for the cooks in the kitchen to prepare the order. In the case of a takeout order, the employee who took the order gives the customer their best estimate of when the food will be ready. There is no tracking of order status today.

The desired future state will incorporate online ordering, but that could mean several things. The overarching solution—letting a customer place an order online and then receive the food—remains constant regardless of how much automation you implement. You will minimally need to introduce one new system: an online ordering website. From there, you could define the solution's boundaries in several possible ways.

1. The simplest solution is a mainly manual process whereby the customer submits an order online, which is sent to a restaurant employee who then enters it into the current order placement system.

2. A semiautomated solution could let customers order meals online and then send those orders to the restaurant order placement system. However, customers would not be able to pay online or receive status updates following order placement.

3. The ultimate, fully automated solution would let customers order all menu items online, dynamically update the menu as items are purchased, permit online payment and order placement to the restaurant, accept delivery requests, and provide the customer with order updates. This would bring additional systems into the project's scope beyond the core online ordering site: payment processing, delivery services, and order tracking.

The solution boundary you select will be based on your business objectives, product vision, constraints (such as security requirements for online payments), timeline, and funding. Consider asking the key stakeholders to describe the smallest "thing" to implement that would meet their objectives. Refining the initial simple solution concept into a richer description will establish how much of the solution remains manual and how much will be automated via new or existing systems.

Clear solution boundaries help the team evaluate new functionality requests to determine to which system they should belong, if any. For the restaurant scenario, the concise solution statement is: "A fully automated online ordering and payment process with integration to third-party delivery and automated order tracking services."

Setting the Context

Once the BA has refined the solution concept, they must position each new system within the company's existing software environment. Start with any available documentation, such as a systems catalog or a system architecture diagram (Lucidchart 2022a). From there, the BA can create a *context diagram* for each new system being built (Weilkiens 2007, Wiegers and Beatty 2013). Figure 2.5 shows a partial context diagram for the restaurant's new online ordering site. A context diagram begins with the system of interest shown in a circle at the center of the diagram. The circle represents the system boundary. The context diagram provides no insight into the internals of that system, just its immediate environment.

A customer will interact with the online ordering site to view menu items, select some items to build an order, and place their order with a valid payment method. To implement the desired full automation, you'll need to integrate the new online ordering site with the existing menu repository and restaurant order placement systems. Additionally, you'll need to connect with an external system for online payment processing. Show all those *external entities* that will interact with the central system in rectangles outside the circle. Finally, the context diagram shows the data that moves between each entity and the system using arrows called *flows*. Label each flow with a high-level description of the data: menu items, payment information, and so forth.

The context diagram delineates the scope of a single system, which could include both automated and manual operations. External entities outside the circle aren't part of that system, although they could be built as part of the same project. Each external system would have its own context diagram to show its system boundary and environment. As the project progresses and the expectations of a release are better understood, the BA may discover more external entities to which the system will connect.

As with other BA techniques, the context diagram is a useful tool to engage with stakeholders to reach a common and accurate mindset. The resultant diagram

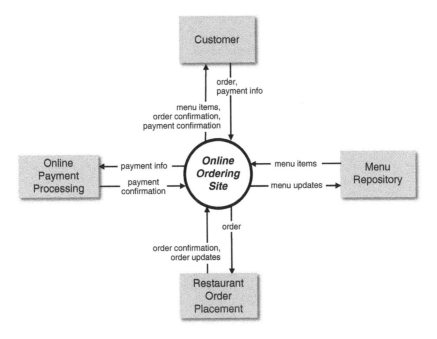

Figure 2.5 *A context diagram shows the immediate environment of the restaurant's new online ordering site.*

formalizes the system boundaries; creating or reviewing it collaboratively can expose potential issues and help resolve misunderstandings.

Expanding the Ecosystem

A context diagram identifies the user classes, hardware devices, and any other systems that interact with a product. However, it only shows the direct connections between our system of interest and those external entities. An *ecosystem map* goes beyond the immediate context of a single system (Beatty and Chen 2012). It depicts the overall solution view, including all systems in a given application domain—or even an entire company—along with the high-level data flows between them. The ecosystem map can help you understand any upstream or downstream impacts you are making on data that the systems exchange.

Figure 2.6 shows an ecosystem map for the restaurant online ordering example. It shows that the desired solution of full automation extends beyond the new online ordering site and its immediate connections. The solution also will involve enhancements to the existing restaurant order placement system to integrate with a new order tracking system and an external third-party delivery application.

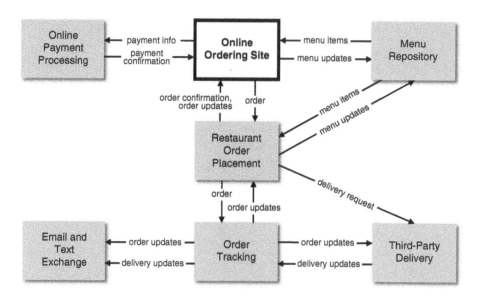

Figure 2.6 *An ecosystem map shows how the restaurant's current and future systems are interconnected.*

To create an ecosystem map, first list the systems in your solution domain. If you don't have a full system list, start with your system of interest and its direct connections. From there, look at each connecting system and its additional connections, showing each system in a box. Move outward until you've covered the entire solution domain.

Next, examine the systems to determine which of them exchange data. Look for both synchronous (API calls) and asynchronous (message-based) integrations, as well as file-based and direct database connections. Link the interrelated systems with arrows indicating each data flow's direction, as in the context diagram.

Complete the ecosystem map with a high-level description of the data that's shared through each connection. Combining the ecosystem map with the context diagram shows both who is using the target system and the overall multisystem view. An ecosystem map has good reuse potential for multiple projects and products within an organization.

Applying the Solution's Boundaries

Once the BA and the team have defined the solution's boundaries, they'll be valuable throughout the project's life for scope definition, product roadmap definition, and release planning. An extensive solution with full online ordering automation could take many months to complete. In iterative projects, the team will break the full implementation into a series of releases or development increments, each of which provides a useful portion of the overall solution. This strategy allows the business to begin achieving its objectives before all the functionality is completed.

To quickly attract those customers who will place orders only online, the team's first release might include building just the online ordering site and integrating it with the existing menu repository and order placement systems. The customer would still have to pick up and pay for the order in person. Subsequent releases would incrementally add functionality to the overall online ordering process. Table 2.1 shows how the ultimate solution could be realized through several development increments and product releases.

Table 2.1 *Example release objectives*

Release	Release objective
1	Build online ordering site and integrate it with existing menu repository and restaurant order placement systems.
2	Add online payment processing to permit payment at time of order placement.
3	Implement order tracking and integrate with third-party delivery services.
4	Provide automated order and delivery updates to the customer.

Analyze each interface in an ecosystem map or context diagram to elicit external interface requirements and constraints. For example, a third-party delivery system likely has defined technical interfaces to which all users must conform. Those interfaces constrain how the order placement system can integrate to the third-party delivery product.

As new requirements arise, use the product vision, business objectives, and solution boundaries to determine whether each requested requirement should be implemented. Suppose you get a request to integrate the order placement system with one or more third-party ordering systems. Based on the current solution boundaries, that capability is out of scope. It could be funded by a separate project. Alternatively, management might opt to broaden this project's scope to address that additional need, providing extra resources and time as needed (this is just a little joke we like to make).

Clearly defined solution boundaries and models of the connections help the BA explain the need for certain functionality. Perhaps someone asks why the online ordering site needs to update the menu repository, as shown in Figure 2.6. Since the order placement system updates the menu repository during meal preparation, must the online ordering site do it as well?

Well, if the ordering site doesn't update the menu repository as soon as a customer places an order, the menu on the website would be out of date, even if only briefly, having no knowledge of current inventory levels. Suppose someone ordered the last one of some item, making it out of stock even though the meal was not yet prepared. If the menu repository weren't updated immediately, another customer could then order that same item but not receive it, thereby annoying them. (Karl has had this experience; he was annoyed.) Using the business objectives, solution boundaries, and ecosystem map, the BA can defend why each requirement belongs in the solution.

You can also use the solution's boundaries to decide which product component should own which pieces of functionality. Allocating requirements appropriately to systems, subsystems, and people is important both for business information systems and for complex products that include both hardware and software elements. Analyzing data inputs and outputs indicates which systems or functions produce certain data objects and which consume them.

By refining the solution concept to a defined set of components and boundaries, the BA can ensure that the solution scope—including new development, enhancements, integrations, and manual operations—is well understood and communicated to all stakeholders.

Related Practices

Practice #2. Define business objectives.

Practice #8. Assess data concepts and relationships.

Next Steps

1. If you haven't already done so, work with your stakeholders to make sure everyone understands the boundaries around the solution the team is creating. Refer to your business objectives and identify the minimal change needed to meet those objectives.

2. Create a context diagram and an ecosystem map to get the full view of your solution's components and boundaries. Look for existing examples of these artifacts that can be updated as appropriate.

3. Use the context diagram and ecosystem map to evaluate your currently requested functionality. Confirm that it really belongs to your current project based on the defined solution's boundaries. If it does not, defer those requests to a future project or redefine the solution's boundaries.

4. Examine the ecosystem map to identify groups or systems that don't connect directly to your product but could require changes because of the data that your solution exchanges with other related systems. Work with the owners of those connected systems to make sure everyone understands and commits to the necessary modifications.

| Practice #4 | Identify and characterize stakeholders. |

Every project has people who care about it: its stakeholders. A *stakeholder* is an individual or group that is actively involved in a project, is affected by it, or can influence its direction. The interests of all the stakeholders intersect in the requirements activities (Wiegers 2022).

Consultant and author Tim Lister describes project success as "meeting the set of all requirements and constraints held as expectations by key stakeholders." Those stakeholders provide the information a BA needs to understand the business problem or opportunity. The right stakeholders can describe the current state and the changes needed to migrate to an improved future state. Their input allows a BA to define the capabilities and characteristics of an appropriate solution and to validate the proposed solution.

It's important to identify the project's significant stakeholder groups early on and determine how best to engage with them. Overlooking stakeholders can lead to requirements gaps or unknown constraints that are disruptive when they're finally discovered. Certain stakeholders set the project's direction and hold authority over major decisions. Others don't provide any input; they merely get what they get. Most stakeholder groups lie somewhere between these extremes along a spectrum of influence and engagement. It's important to identify those stakeholders who are most heavily involved with making various decisions (see Practice #5, "Identify empowered decision makers").

Simply identifying and characterizing your stakeholder categories isn't sufficient. You also must select appropriate representatives of those groups to participate in requirements activities. Even then, stakeholder issues can cause requirements problems. Missing roles, absent participants, and ineffective surrogates can lead to requirements errors that you'll need to fix later at greater expense.

The Quest for Stakeholders

A project's business objectives and vision statement provide a starting point in your stakeholder search. The first sentence of the sample vision statement from Practice #2, "Define business objectives," began as follows:

> *For* business analysts, product managers, product owners, requirements engineers, user representatives, developers, testers, and other team members *who* are responsible for requirements development and management activities....

The list of people following the opening keyword *For* is an initial set of stakeholders.

As you continue the hunt, cast a wide net to reduce the chance of overlooking a significant group. To save time, you might begin with a stakeholder catalog accumulated from previous projects. Scan through that catalog to see if any of those same groups are relevant to your current project. Building a stakeholder catalog incrementally from one project to the next provides a valuable reusable asset to use as a starting point the next time. An organization chart can help you detect other potential stakeholders.

You can also refer to a comprehensive list of typical stakeholder categories to look for possibilities, like the one in Table 2.2 (Wiegers and Beatty 2013). Some stakeholders are found within the development team, others work elsewhere in the developing organization, and still more lie somewhere outside the developing organization.

Some stakeholders may be primarily interested in the project itself, others in the solution the project delivers. For instance, users don't care much about how a product is built if it lets them do their work efficiently and without much frustration. When you're searching for stakeholders, consider questions like these (Leffingwell 2011).

- Who has influence or control over the project's budget and schedule?
- Who can articulate the project's business objectives?
- Who will be using the product directly? Indirectly?
- Who is responsible for other systems or projects that yours will affect or will affect yours?
- Who could have legal, compliance, regulatory, or process influence?
- Who manages the business relationships with customers, suppliers, and contractors?
- Whose business processes would the system affect?
- Who is expected to supply any data needed by the solution?
- Who would know about any pertinent project, product, or process constraints?

As you accumulate a stakeholder list, ask other stakeholders to review it. They often know of someone else who should be included.

Table 2.2 *Some common potential software project stakeholders and where they're likely to be found*

Location	Category	
Development team	Application architect	Infrastructure analyst
	Business analyst	Product manager
	Data analyst	Product owner
	Database administrator	Project manager
	Database designer	Quality assurance
	Developer	Software designer
	Documentation writer	Tester
	Hardware engineer	User experience designer
Inside the developing organization	Company owner	Marketing
	Compliance	Operations support
	Contract manager	People responsible for connected systems
	Development manager	Portfolio architect
	Executive sponsor	Process analyst
	Information architect	Program manager
	Infrastructure support	Project management office
	Installer	Sales
	Legal	Security analyst
	Maintainer	Training
	Manufacturing	
Outside the developing organization	Auditor	Government agency
	Beta tester	Indirect user
	Business management	Materials supplier
	Certifier	Procurement staff
	Compliance auditor	Purchaser
	Consultant	Regulatory body
	Contracting office	Shareholder
	Contractor	Software supplier
	Customer management	Subject matter expert
	Direct user	Venture capitalist
	General public	

Stakeholders, Customers, and User Classes

People sometimes use the terms *stakeholder*, *customer*, and *user* interchangeably. However, as you can see from Table 2.2, only certain stakeholders are customers, and only certain customers will use the product. Some customers present solution requirements, evaluate candidate products, supply data, or acquire a product but never touch it themselves. Other nonusers of an information system still could be stakeholders because business operations include manual actions as well as computer tasks. A software system could have an impact on those manual operations. Steven Blais (2012) refers to this set of both system users and affected nonusers collectively as *process workers*.

Don't regard your users as a monolithic group: "the user." Nearly every product has multiple—sometimes many—*user classes*. Members of various user classes may differ in the features they use, tasks they perform, frequency of use, location, access or privilege level, education or experience level, and in other ways. Many users will interact with an information system directly. Indirect users provide inputs to it or receive outputs from it but don't interact with the system themselves. User classes could also be other software systems or hardware devices that obtain services from your product.

Treat each user class as a separate stakeholder subcategory because the BA will need to work with representatives of each class to understand their needs. Some overlap of requirements across user classes is common.

Certain user classes may be favored over others because their interests more strongly coincide with the initiative's business objectives (Gause and Lawrence 1999). Those groups should carry more weight than others regarding decisions about requirements priorities, proposed requirement changes, and similar matters. Identifying the favored user classes helps you resolve priority and functionality conflicts that arise across classes.

As an example of different user classes for a product, consider a hypothetical publishing platform called Speak-Out.biz, on which authors can post articles on any topic they like. Readers can view articles, comment on articles, and subscribe to their favorite authors. Authors can submit their articles to any of numerous publications that aggregate articles on diverse themes. Editors select whether to include submitted articles in their publications. This brief description names or implies several user classes for Speak-Out.biz:

- Author
- Reader
- Publication Editor
- Administrator

Each type of user has various tasks they wish to perform on the platform, certain usage privileges, and particular functional and quality expectations of the product. If you were launching such a publishing platform, you'd want to characterize the various user classes and then seek suitable representatives to understand each group's requirements and constraints. We'll revisit Speak-Out.biz in some upcoming practices.

Characterizing Stakeholders

Early in the project, perform an analysis to understand who your stakeholders are, each group's interests in the project, their influence over it, and their expectations and concerns (Gottesdiener 2005, Lucidchart 2022b). Questions like the following will provide a rich understanding of each stakeholder group (McManus 2005, Wiegers 2022).

- Who are they? How many of them are there?
- Where are they? What's the best way to communicate with them?
- What roles do they play with respect to the project?
- How much power or influence do they have over the project?
- What are their interests, concerns, and fears?
- What benefits do they wish to receive from the product? What are their needs, expectations, and success criteria?
- What information can they provide regarding operations, technology, data, or other areas?
- What do they need to know about the project?
- For users, how will they use the product?

Table 2.3 illustrates a simple template with information to record for each stakeholder profile, using one of the stakeholders from Speak-Out.biz as an example. Your organization could accumulate these profiles from multiple projects into a reusable, enterprise-level stakeholder catalog. Stakeholder profiles go into section 3.1 of the vision and scope document template, which was shown in Figure 2.2. If you already have a stakeholder catalog, you can just point to the appropriate entries in that section of the vision and scope document rather than duplicating the information.

Table 2.3 *Portion of a sample stakeholder profile for Speak-Out.biz*

Stakeholder	Roles	Interests	Influence	Needs	Concerns
Author	Writes, edits, and posts articles; tracks statistics and earnings	Interest = High; reaching a broad audience; generating revenue from articles	Power = Low: can request features and report problems or abuse	Easy-to-use text editor; submitting articles to publications; customizable statistics reports	Integrity of posted articles; long-term stability of platform

With your stakeholder catalog in hand, identify individuals who can accurately represent the interests of each stakeholder group and agree upon how they will engage with the BA and other team members. Make sure those representatives will have the bandwidth to contribute to the initiative in the necessary time frame. It can be more challenging to find and interact with stakeholders outside the developing organization than with internal people. However, their participation may be critical because of their authority, responsibilities, control over resources, or political, legal, or regulatory influence.

Consider whether each group is a collaborative partner in development, can make final decisions about certain aspects of the project, should be consulted for their expertise on specific issues, or just needs to be informed of progress and decisions that affect them (Leffingwell 2011). Some teams create a *RACI matrix* to identify stakeholder roles and their responsibilities with respect to the project. The RACI matrix shows which stakeholders are **R**esponsible, **A**ccountable, **C**onsulted, or **I**nformed (Morris 2022).

Make sure you know who is speaking for each stakeholder community. For the vital role of user representative, the *product champion* approach works well in many situations (Wiegers and Beatty 2013). A product champion is a designated and empowered key representative of a specific user class. Product champions work closely with BAs through interviews, workshops, prototype evaluations, and other collaborative activities to elicit and validate requirements. A product champion serves as the literal voice of the customer for a specific category of users. If you can't engage with actual user representatives directly, someone must still speak for the needs of each user class as a proxy.

The time spent on stakeholder analysis early on might seem like a distraction from real software work. Not so—it *is* the real work of ensuring that you engage the right participants in a collaborative effort that builds a solid base for success.

Related Practices

Practice #1.   Understand the problem before converging on a solution.

Practice #2.   Define business objectives.

Practice #3.   Define the solution's boundaries.

Practice #5.   Identify empowered decision makers.

Practice #6.   Understand what users need to do with the solution.

Practice #13. Prioritize the requirements.

Next Steps

1. Examine Table 2.2 for any stakeholders for your initiative that might have been overlooked.

2. Characterize each of your significant stakeholder groups so that you can identify appropriate representatives and agree on how to engage with them.

3. Set up a template format for a stakeholder catalog and begin populating it with your stakeholder information for this project. If your organization works on projects that have recurrent stakeholders, establish a mechanism to maintain and reuse this catalog on future initiatives.

4. Identify your significant user classes. Note any user classes that are favored over others. Make sure it's clear who presents the requirements, constraints, dependencies, and risks for each user class. Confirm that those individuals have the knowledge and authority to perform their representation role well.

Practice #5	Identify empowered decision makers.

Every project faces a continual stream of decisions large and small. Individual team members can make many decisions locally and informally; other issues have a far broader impact. Making a considered decision about a requirements issue often demands obtaining input from multiple sources, having appropriate stakeholders assess the options, and communicating the outcome—and the reasons for it—to all affected communities. Common classes of requirements-related decisions include these:

- Resolving conflicting requirements within a user class and across user classes
- Prioritizing requirements of various types
- Resolving conflicting priorities among different stakeholders
- Adjusting priorities as new needs come along and project realities change
- Making trade-off choices between conflicting quality attributes
- Defining the number of development increments or releases and the scope of each one
- Determining which new or changed requirements to incorporate into development plans (product backlog management)
- Deciding when and how to modify the scope of a planned development increment, a product release, or the entire project

Some organizations—and individuals—are better at making decisions than others. Karl used to work at a company in which decision-making was sluggish because no one wanted anybody to be uncomfortable with the outcome. That's not practical. As a colleague pointed out, "This company is not a democracy." Someone must choose among the options and set directions so that everyone can work toward the shared objectives. It was frustrating to deal with managers who vacillated, never reaching closure on issues that were appropriate for their level. Karl had more respect for managers who *would* make a decision, even if he didn't always agree with it.

It's important to determine who the decision makers will be for various requirements issues. The initiative's leaders should do this before the group confronts their first significant decision. Identifying the decision makers ensures that decisions can be made at the lowest possible level. Issues are resolved more quickly when decisions are made locally than when small matters are escalated to a higher level. Each group also should agree upon how they will reach their conclusions—that is, which decision rule or rules they'll apply—and the path forward if they're unable to resolve an issue.

Who Makes the Call?

The right people to make each category of decision depends on the situation. Major scope issues that affect schedules, resources, and existing commitments will involve senior managers or executives. Those managers could be in the developing organization, a customer organization, marketing, or combinations of those. A single requirement change could have a big ripple effect if it forces revisions to multiple interconnected elements. Representatives from all the affected components need to know about the decision outcome, even if they don't all participate in making it.

Identifying the decision makers for requirements issues is a part of stakeholder analysis. Input from those stakeholders whose interests align most closely with the project's business objectives, such as favored user classes, should carry the most weight. Stakeholders who impose constraints—including scope, resource, regulatory, legal, business policy, or technical restrictions—may override functionality requests from other groups that conflict with the constraints. Agreeing on which stakeholders contribute most heavily to which important decisions helps the group reach conclusions more quickly and perhaps with less rancor.

Each decision-making group should identify a decision leader to coordinate their activities. The idea is not to add bureaucratic overhead, but rather to provide clear lines of responsibility, authority, and accountability. A group of people might think they have the authority to make decisions about a certain range of issues. But if someone else can override their choices, then, in effect, that group is merely an advisory body; the other "someone" is the ultimate decision maker. The decision leader makes all those roles and responsibilities clear to avoid delays, uncertainty, revisited decisions, and hard feelings.

On typical agile projects, the product owner (PO) is the decision leader for requirements-related issues. This is consistent with the PO's responsibilities for creating, prioritizing, and managing items in the product backlog to guide the team toward achieving the desired outcome (Agile Alliance 2022a). The PO's central role is sometimes described as being the "single wringable neck" in case things go awry (Bernstein 2016). We hope that's meant to be tongue in cheek.

One large project, for which Karl was the lead BA, assembled a user requirements team with representatives from four user classes: product champions, as described in Practice #4, "Identify and characterize stakeholders." The largest and most diverse user class required additional representatives from several subgroups to cover the breadth of needs. When requests from the subgroups didn't agree, the product champion for that overall user class was fully empowered to make the choice. And he did! The other participants respected the product champion's experience, wisdom, and conclusions. Having a few carefully selected and empowered user representatives who could make requirements decisions on behalf of their respective communities made life much easier for the three BAs.

How Do They Decide?

Too often, when people begin to collaborate on some initiative, they don't discuss exactly *how* they're going to work together. An important—and sometimes adversarial—aspect of collaboration is making high-impact decisions that influence the project's direction. When Karl began his first experience coauthoring a book, he and his coauthor spent a lot of time planning how they would work together, including how they would resolve conflicts regarding how to handle a particular topic. Those involved with every multiperson activity should have this same discussion before they confront their first conflict.

Decisions related to requirements should use the business requirements as their North Star. Rely on your business objectives to make choices that keep the work focused on delivering the desired value. Some teams write their business objectives, vision statement, and scope descriptions on a large poster. They bring this poster to discussions about requirements (or present a refresher slide show to open virtual meetings) to help them choose the appropriate course of action. These actions remind everyone of the goals they're working together to achieve.

The objective of all decision-making is to expeditiously and respectfully reach closure on issues based on accurate information, thoughtful analysis, and honest negotiation. The process for making a decision is called a *decision rule*. There are numerous possible decision rules, including these (Gottesdiener 2002, Pichler 2016):

Unanimous Vote. The participants vote on the options, and all must vote the same way to resolve the issue. It can be time-consuming, and sometimes impossible, to lead a group of people with diverse interests to all agree on a given outcome. If achieved, unanimity provides the strongest group commitment to the decision. An outside facilitator can help a group achieve either unanimous agreement or consensus when buy-in across the board is essential.

Consensus. All participants agree that they can live with the group's decision, although they may vary in their commitment to it and their comfort level with it. Consensus is not as strong an agreement as unanimous voting. Reaching a consensus often requires considerable discussion and compromise. It takes longer than a simple vote, but the consensus-building process achieves more solid buy-in to significant decisions.

Plurality Vote. The decision makers vote on the options, and the one that receives the most votes is selected as the decision. Plurality (sometimes called majority) voting is most appropriate for low-impact decisions that have several clear options.

Decision Leader Decides. A single individual can make decisions more quickly than a group can. Depending on the decision leader's knowledge and expertise regarding the issue, the leader can either solicit input from others or reach a conclusion on their own. Soliciting others' input is more collaborative and promotes stronger commitment to the outcome by those whom the decision affects. If people feel that their voice was not heard before the decision leader set the direction, they'll be less satisfied with the result.

Delegation. The leader appoints someone else who has the appropriate knowledge to decide. The leader should not use delegation to avoid responsibility for whatever course of action the delegate chooses. Delegating the decision to someone else demonstrates trust in the delegate's experience and judgment. However, if the decision leader overrides the delegate's decision, that undermines the trust and effectively reverts to the Decision Leader Decides rule.

No single decision rule applies universally to situations; there's no "correct" rule. Nonetheless, every group that must make decisions about requirements issues should agree on its process—and then follow it.

What Happens Following the Decision?

The most important outputs from any meeting or discussion are action items to pursue, issues to address, and decisions that were made. Decisions have a way of resurfacing when someone down the road isn't aware of the outcome, doesn't agree with it, or doesn't understand why it was made. The team should record its significant decisions along with the rationale behind each one. This record makes the decision outcome available to others who weren't involved in the discussion. The team should discuss how to justify the decision to others who might challenge it.

The results of nonlocal decisions also need to be communicated to those whom the decision affects. Without clear and timely communication, team members might implement requirements that were canceled or deferred, misunderstand priorities, or otherwise work at cross purposes. When project participants understand the reasoning behind significant decisions, they can better collaborate toward common ends.

Related Practices

Practice #3. Define the solution's boundaries.

Practice #4. Identify and characterize stakeholders.

Practice #9. Elicit and evaluate quality attributes.

Practice #13. Prioritize the requirements.

Practice #20. Manage changes to requirements effectively.

Next Steps

1. Review the common requirements decisions listed at the beginning of this section and identify those that apply to your situation. Does your project encounter any other requirements-related decisions that are not on that list?

2. Is it clear who the decision makers would be for each category from the previous step? If not, identify them now.

3. If you have groups who are involved in the major requirements decisions from the previous steps, determine whether they have selected appropriate decision rules. If they have, find out if they apply them regularly and whether those rules work well. If they don't have decision rules in mind, help them make that selection.

4. Establish a convention regarding how your project or program will record and communicate its key decisions to those stakeholders who need to be informed about them.

Chapter 3

Requirements Elicitation

The first step in dealing with requirements is to get some. People often speak of "gathering requirements," as though it were a simple collection process: The requirements are sitting around in people's heads, and the business analyst merely asks for them and writes them down. It's never that simple. In reality, stakeholders begin with random fragments of information: dissatisfaction with their current systems, bits of functionality they want, tasks to perform, important pieces of data, and ideas of what screen displays might look like.

Requirements elicitation is a better term for this foundational activity. To elicit something means to draw it forth or bring it out, particularly something that's hidden or latent. The *Merriam-Webster Thesaurus* (2022) says, "*elicit* usually implies some effort or skill in drawing forth a response." That skill is a significant asset that a business analyst brings to software development. Requirements elicitation does involve collection, but it also involves exploration, discovery, and invention. The BA guides this imaginative journey, working with diverse stakeholders to understand the problem and then define a satisfactory solution. The BA looks for potential requirements from many sources, including these:

- User representatives and many other stakeholders
- Documentation about business processes, current systems, and competing products
- Laws, regulations, and business policies
- Existing systems, which may or may not be documented
- User problem reports, help desk records, and support staff

An experienced BA exploits multiple techniques for elicitation, choosing the appropriate tool for a particular situation. Factors to consider when selecting elicitation methods include the types of information needed; who has that information, where those people are located, and their availability; the effort that the method requires; the budget and time available; the development team's life cycle model and methodologies; and the cultures of the developing and customer organizations (IIBA 2015).

This book does not go into elicitation techniques in detail, as those are thoroughly described in other resources (e.g., Davis 2005, Robertson and Robertson 2013, Wiegers and Beatty 2013, IIBA 2015). Table 3.1 lists several commonly used elicitation activities and the typical participants.

Table 3.1 *Some common requirements elicitation techniques*

Participants	Activities
Business analyst	• Data mining and analysis • Document analysis • Existing product and process analysis • System interface analysis • User interface analysis
Business analyst and stakeholders	• Brainstorming • Collaboration tools such as wikis and discussion forums • Facilitated group workshops • Focus groups • Interviews • Mind mapping • Observing users at work • Process modeling • Prototyping • Questionnaires and surveys • Scenario analysis

This chapter describes four core practices that are particularly valuable for eliciting both functional and nonfunctional requirements:

Practice #6. Understand what users need to do with the solution.

Practice #7. Identify events and responses.

Practice #8. Assess data concepts and relationships.

Practice #9. Elicit and evaluate quality attributes.

Practice #6 Understand what users need to do with the solution.

If you were holding a requirements elicitation discussion with some users about a new information system, which of these questions do you think would yield the greatest insights?

- What do you want?
- What are your requirements?
- What do you want the system to do?
- What features would you like to see in the system?
- What do you need to do with the solution?

We favor the final question. While the first four questions can provide a good starting point to ask *why* a stakeholder wants those things, they all inquire about the solution, not the user's problems, needs, or goals. Focusing on features can lead the team to implement incomplete functionality that doesn't let users do all the things they must do. The feature-centered mindset also can lead to building functionality that seems like a good idea but goes unused because it doesn't directly relate to user tasks. Regardless of your development approach, if you don't understand what the users need to do with the features they request, you might release a product that you must rework later.

Karl once saw the limitations of elicitation questions that focus on the solution. A company held a daylong workshop with about sixty participants to brainstorm ideas for a large new commercial product. They stapled together the output from their six subgroups and called it a requirements specification. But it wasn't. It was a mishmash of functionality fragments, feature descriptions, user tasks, data objects, and performance expectations, along with extraneous information, all stirred together with no structure or organization. Simply asking people to imagine what they wanted to see in the new product didn't produce actionable requirements knowledge. Much more requirements development work was needed following the workshop.

Focusing on Usage

The question "What do you need to do with the solution?" is a more effective opening for discussing requirements. By understanding what the users need to do, the BA can deduce just what functionality is needed. A usage-centric approach makes it more likely that the solution will satisfy user needs, incorporating the necessary capabilities without wasting development effort on unneeded functions (Wiegers 2022).

Stories, scenarios, and use cases are variations on a common theme: asking users to describe an interaction they might have with a software system or a business to achieve some goal (Alexander and Maiden 2004). These descriptions of user goals and the interactions that lead to achieving them constitute the user requirements. User requirements appear in the middle section of the requirements information model in Figure 1.1, as reproduced in Figure 3.1. The user requirements should align with the business objectives from the vision and scope document and contribute to solving an identified business problem.

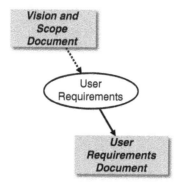

Figure 3.1 *User requirements lie between business requirements and solution requirements.*

Eliciting User Requirements

A person doesn't launch an application to use a particular feature; they launch it to do something. It's difficult for users to articulate their "requirements," but they can easily describe how they might perform a business activity. During an elicitation discussion, the BA might ask a user representative, "Please describe a session you might have with the product we're talking about. What would you be trying to accomplish? How do you imagine your dialogue with the system would go?" A description of a single interactive session like this is called a *scenario*.

A scenario identifies a sequence of steps that define a task to achieve a specific intent (Alexander and Maiden 2004). When you ask a user to describe a scenario, they'll usually begin with the most typical or frequent activity they perform. This is sometimes called the normal flow, main flow, main success scenario, or happy path. From that initial scenario, the BA and user can then explore *alternative* scenarios (or flows), variations that also lead to a successful outcome. They can also discuss *exceptions*, possible conditions that could prevent a scenario from concluding successfully.

An effective way to organize these related scenarios is in the form of *use cases* (Cockburn 2001, Kulak and Guiney 2004). A use case structures all this information according to a template, which is described in the next section. The use case technique helps the team acquire and organize the mass of requirements information that any sizable system involves. If an elicitation participant says "I want to *<do something>*" or "I need to be able to *<do something>*," the *<do something>* likely is a use case.

The various user classes will have different use cases, different things they need to accomplish with the solution. That's why it's a good idea to conduct group elicitation activities with members of each user class separately. As an example, Table 3.2 lists a few use cases for each of the user classes named earlier for the hypothetical Speak-Out.biz publication platform in Practice #4, "Identify and characterize stakeholders."

Table 3.2 *Some use cases for several Speak-Out.biz user classes*

User class	Use cases
Author	Draft an Article
	Edit an Article
	Publish an Article
	Submit an Article to a Publication
	View Article Statistics
Reader	Read an Article
	Comment on an Article
	Subscribe to an Author
Publication Editor	Create a New Publication
	Accept or Reject a Submitted Article
	Reply to an Author
Administrator	Respond to a Reader Complaint
	Suspend an Author's Account

Each use case name is a concise statement that clearly indicates the user's goal, the outcome of value that the user wishes to achieve. Notice that all the use cases in Table 3.2 begin with a definitive action verb. This is a standard use case naming convention.

Agile projects often rely on *user stories* as a technique for discussing system capabilities. According to agile expert Mike Cohn (2004), "A user story describes functionality that will be valuable to either a user or purchaser of the system or software." A user story is intentionally brief, a starting point for further exploration of its details so that developers can learn enough to implement the story. User stories conform to a simple pattern, such as this one:

As a *<type of user>*, I want to *<perform some task>* so that I can *<achieve some goal>*.

Stories that focus on what users need to do with the solution, rather than on bits of system functionality, can serve the goal of usage-centric requirements exploration. Here's a user story we might hear from a Speak-Out.biz author:

As an author, I want to view the page-view statistics for my published articles so that I can see which topics my readers enjoy the most.

This story addresses a piece of the functionality for the final use case shown for the Author user class in Table 3.2, View Article Statistics. The user story format offers the advantages of naming the user class and describing the intent. That information would appear in a use case specification, but it's helpful to see it right up front like this.

There are ongoing debates about whether use cases are appropriate—or even allowed—for agile development. This isn't the place to rehash those debates, but the short answer is: They are (Leffingwell 2011). Both use cases and user stories have their advantages and limitations (Bergman 2010). Both can be used to explore what users need to accomplish with the solution.

One of the BA's challenges is to examine a particular scenario that describes a single usage session and consider how to generalize it to encompass a group of logically related scenarios. That is, the BA moves up the abstraction scale from a specific scenario to a more general use case. Similarly, the BA on an agile project might see that a set of related user stories can be abstracted into a larger *epic* that needs to be implemented over several iterations.

At other times, elicitation participants might begin with a complex usage description that the BA realizes should be split into multiple use cases. Those individual use cases often can be implemented, and executed, independently, although several could perhaps be chained together during execution to carry out a larger task. On an agile project, a user story that's too large to implement in a single iteration is split into several smaller stories. Moving between levels of abstraction like this is a natural part of exploring user requirements.

Use cases facilitate top-down thinking, describing multiple scenarios and fleshing out the details of the user–system interactions. Use cases provide a context for organizing related pieces of information. Epics perform an analogous top-down function on agile projects. User stories describe smaller user goals or pieces of system functionality without much context or detail. Stories generally are smaller than use cases, describing slices of functionality that can be implemented in a single development iteration. Related user stories can be grouped together and abstracted into an appropriate use case or an epic. Any approach can be effective—use cases or user stories, top-down or bottom-up—provided the focus stays on usage.

Anatomy of a Use Case

Unlike the simple user story format, a use case specification follows a rich template like the one in Figure 3.2 (Wiegers and Beatty 2013). You may download this template from the website that accompanies this book. A collection of use case descriptions could serve as the contents of the user requirements document ("container") that appears in Figure 3.1. Nothing says that you must complete this full template for each of your use cases. Write in whatever level of detail will clearly communicate the use case information to those who must validate, implement, or write tests based on it.

Use Case Element	Description
ID and Name	Give each use case a unique identifier and a descriptive name.
Primary Actor	Identify the actor (user role) who initiates the use case and derives the principal benefit from it.
Secondary Actors	Identify other users or systems that participate in performing the use case.
Description	Provide a brief description of the use case in just a few sentences.
Trigger	Identify the event or action that initiates the use case's execution.
Preconditions	State any prerequisites that must be met before the use case can begin.
Postconditions	State conditions that are true after the use case is successfully completed.
Normal Flow	The core of a use case specification describes how the user visualizes interacting with the system to accomplish the goal. List the steps in the dialog that takes place between the primary actor, the system, and any other systems or actors that participate in the normal flow scenario.
Alternative Flows	Describe any alternative ways the use case might be performed and still satisfy the postconditions. Alternative flows often involve branching away from the normal flow at some step and then perhaps rejoining it.
Exceptions	Identify conditions for each flow that could terminate the scenario before it completes successfully. Describe how the system should respond or help the user resolve the problem.
Priority	State the relative priority of this use case compared to others.
Business Rules	Point to any business rules that influence how this use case is implemented or executed.
Assumptions	State any known assumptions that people are making with respect to this use case.

Figure 3.2 *A rich use case specification template.*

Applying Usage-centric Requirements Information

User requirements serve as a starting point for several subsequent activities. Both use cases and user stories need to be further elaborated into a set of functional requirements, which is what developers implement. This step takes place whether a BA does it analytically and documents the resultant details or whether each developer does it in their head on the fly (not the recommended approach).

Use cases and user stories both facilitate starting testing early in the development cycle. If a BA derives functional requirements from a use case and a tester derives tests, you now have two representations of requirements knowledge that you can compare. That comparison can reveal requirements errors, ambiguities, and omissions. See Practice #18, "Review and test the requirements," for more on this topic. Documenting how the system should handle exceptions lets developers build more robust software and helps testers do a more thorough job.

User stories and use cases also lie at the core of requirements prioritization. The deciding stakeholder typically prioritizes user stories or use cases in a sequence that maximizes customer value. The team then fits them into iterations or increments based on the team's available capacity, considering any relevant technical and functional dependencies. While user stories are each prioritized on their own, the individual flows within a use case could have different priorities. You might opt to implement the normal flow and its exceptions in one development increment, and then implement alternative flows and their corresponding exceptions in upcoming increments.

Usage-centric requirements exploration won't reveal behind-the-scenes capabilities, such as a timeout to turn off some device or log out a user after a period of inactivity. Nonetheless, focusing elicitation on understanding what users must do with the system helps the team implement all the necessary—and no unnecessary—functionality. Usage-centric thinking also leads nicely into designing an optimal user experience (Constantine and Lockwood 1999).

Related Practices

Practice #2. Define business objectives.

Practice #4. Identify and characterize stakeholders.

Practice #7. Identify events and responses.

Practice #13. Prioritize the requirements.

Practice #16. Identify and document business rules.

Practice #18. Review and test the requirements.

Next Steps

1. If your team has not explored the tasks that users want to perform with the solution you're building, have conversations with your user representatives to identify their use cases. Explore alternative scenarios along with the normal flow. Make sure to note exceptions and how they should be handled.

2. Try completing the use case template in Figure 3.2 for several of your use cases. How could you simplify the template and still meet the needs of your developers and testers?

3. If your project is employing user stories, try documenting a group of related scenarios both in the use case format and as a set of user stories. Which approach seems most effective and efficient for your team?

| Practice #7 | Identify events and responses. |

As we saw in the previous practice, use cases are an effective way to explore the tasks that users need to accomplish with the help of a software system and identify the functionality needed. Use cases are particularly well suited for interactive systems. Use cases don't fully solve the requirements problem on all types of products, though.

A complementary elicitation technique is to identify the various events that a business or a software system could experience, which trigger some behavior in response. Event analysis is especially effective with real-time or middleware systems in which user–system interactions don't constitute the main product operations. Such applications include software that does most of its work in the background, like an antimalware product.

Products that contain both hardware and software components, whether embedded or host based, also are well suited for event analysis. A complex city intersection is a good example. It involves sensors embedded in the street, cameras, crosswalk buttons, timers, and multiple traffic signals. Inputs from these components—events—stimulate the behaviors that drivers and pedestrians observe at the intersection. There aren't many use cases for either drivers (go straight, turn right, turn left) or pedestrians (cross the street), yet an intersection's system components have a lot going on.

Types of Events

An *event* is a change that takes place in the application's environment that triggers some type of response. As Figure 3.3 and Table 3.3 show, we need to consider three classes of events.

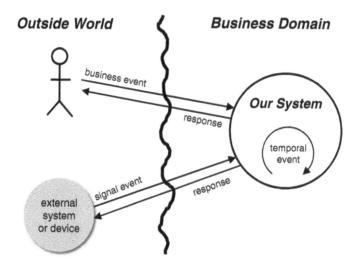

Figure 3.3 *Businesses and systems must respond to several types of events.*

Table 3.3 *Different types of possible events*

Event type	Description
Business	Someone outside the business domain requests a service from the domain. A person or a system in the business domain responds to the service request. The response to a business event often involves initiating an interaction with a software system through a use case.
Signal	A signal event triggers a response when a system receives an input from outside the business domain, such as a control signal from a sensor or a particular data value from another software system.
Temporal	Time-triggered conditions stimulate the system to process some data, generate an output, or perform some other function.

A *business event* originates from the world outside the business domain and crosses the boundary into the business domain (Alexander and Maiden 2004). *Business domain* simply means whatever area your solution applies to, whether it's an actual corporate business, a phone app, a game, a physical device, or anything else. The business event generates some reaction from an entity—human, computer based, or both—inside the domain.

As an example, Karl must renew his automobile registration every two years, which requires his car to pass an emissions test. The business event consists of Karl bringing his car to the testing station and telling the technician that he needs the emissions test performed. The technician responds by taking Karl's renewal application and then beginning the test.

When responding to a business event, someone inside the domain may initiate one or more use cases in a software system. During the emissions test, the technician logs information into their computer system, which also receives and displays the test results from a sensor they plug into the car. If the car passes, the technician completes the process, prints Karl's new registration, and hands him the paperwork and a sticker for the license plate. Mission accomplished!

Signal events originate from a hardware device like a switch or sensor, or they arrive as messages on an incoming communications channel. A signal event, such as an interrupt or a specific data value, notifies the system of the input and triggers some response. The sensor that the technician plugs into Karl's car sends a data stream to the emissions testing application running on their computer, along with a signal when the test is complete. At that point, the host software analyzes the sensor data and reports whether the car passed the test. A system could also generate a signal event when a process completes successfully (or doesn't) and the system needs to notify a user, communicate with another system, or write a data record.

Finally, *temporal events* stimulate a system to perform some action either at a predetermined time or when a specific duration has passed since a previous event took place or a system state was reached. A temporal event triggers the Department of Motor Vehicles to mail Karl a renewal notification two months before his car registration expires. A temporal event could even be a nonevent, in a way. If you've applied for a bank loan and the bank doesn't receive some necessary documentation by a specified date, the bank's system might automatically change the loan application status to "suspended."

How you classify events really isn't that important. The main point is to think about the various events that could take place in your solution's environment and make sure that you identify all the necessary functional and nonfunctional requirements to handle them. Contemplating these three event types might help you recognize more events than initially come to mind.

Specifying Events

You can use various techniques to document the results of an event analysis. The simplest is to list the events that could trigger some system behavior. An antimalware software product's event list could contain entries like these:

- A flash drive is plugged into a USB port (a signal event).

- It's time to initiate a scheduled full-system malware scan (a temporal event).

- One hour has passed since the system last checked for updates to download (a temporal event).

- The computer's administrator initiates a manual malware scan (a business event).

An event list helps with scoping decisions. The people responsible for planning can choose which event processing to incorporate into a specific development iteration or product release.

An *event-response table* provides a more detailed description of possible events and the expected response based on the system's state when it detects each event. Table 3.4 shows a partial event-response table for a home security system. Note that the same event can trigger different responses—or perhaps even no response—depending on the system state at that time.

Table 3.4 *A partial event-response table for a home security system*

Event	System state	Response
User arms system for stay	Disarmed, no open sensors	Change system state to Armed for Stay
User arms system for away	Disarmed, no open sensors	Enable interior motion detectors; initialize countdown timer for exiting the home; change system state to Armed for Away
User arms system for stay or away	Disarmed, open sensor detected	Display open sensor location
User enters correct alarm code	Armed for Away or Armed for Stay	Change system state to Disarmed
User enters incorrect alarm code	Armed for Away or Armed for Stay	Clear alarm code entry display; no state change
Door or window sensor is triggered	Armed for Away or Armed for Stay	Change system state to Intrusion Detected; initiate countdown timer; control panel beeps
Motion detector is triggered	Armed for Away	Change system state to Intrusion Detected; initiate countdown timer; control panel beeps
Motion detector is triggered	Disarmed or Armed for Stay	No response
Countdown timer expires without user entering correct alarm code	Intrusion Detected	Change system state to Alarm Mode; system sounds siren and calls alarm monitoring company
User enters correct alarm code	Intrusion Detected or Alarm Mode	Turn off siren if sounding; change system state to Disarmed
User enters incorrect alarm code	Intrusion Detected	Clear alarm code entry display; countdown timer continues; no state change

An event-response table does not replace written requirements specifications. The table lacks many details that let the developer know exactly how the system is to function. That is, the event-response table summarizes the system behavior at a fairly high level of abstraction. Looking at Table 3.4, several questions come to mind that the table doesn't answer, including these.

- What are the durations of the various countdown timers? Can they be user set? If so, are there minimum and maximum allowed values?

- What exactly does calling the alarm monitoring company involve? Are sounding the siren and calling the only things that happen when the system goes into Alarm Mode? Does the system ever turn off the siren without the user entering the correct alarm code?

- Are any details needed regarding "control panel beeps?" Pattern, frequency, volume, timing? Or will those all be design decisions?

- What all happens upon disarming the system?

- Could any exceptions arise that the system must handle? (Karl's home security system recently went berserk because of an improperly handled exception condition.)

The BA can use an event-response table on agile projects to itemize acceptance criteria, particularly if they are written using the Given-When-Then format (see Practice #18, "Review and test the requirements"). The states become the "givens" or preconditions, each event the "when" or trigger, and the responses the "thens." The team could update the table as they deal with new event and state combinations, or they could start by building a complete table and then plan the development sequence based on that knowledge.

One problem with presenting a lot of information in tabular form is that it's hard to tell if it's complete and accurate. Karl once reviewed a requirements specification that contained a multipage event-response table. Events triggered certain functionality and switched the system from one state to another. The complex table was hard to decipher and verify as being correct and complete.

In this case, Karl found it helpful to represent the table's contents in an alternative, visual form. He drew a *state-transition diagram* that showed the various system states and the events that caused state changes (Wiegers and Beatty 2013). There are several notations and names for similar visual models, including state diagram, state machine diagram, and statechart diagram (Ambler 2005, Beatty and Chen 2012).

As an illustration, Figure 3.4 shows a state-transition diagram for the portion of a home security system described in Table 3.4. Each rectangle represents a possible system state. The arrows indicate allowed transitions that can take place between states. Labels on the arrows indicate the event and/or conditions that trigger a change of state. This model does not explicitly show all the system behaviors that result from an event, which do appear in the event-response table. The two representations—table and diagram—are complementary.

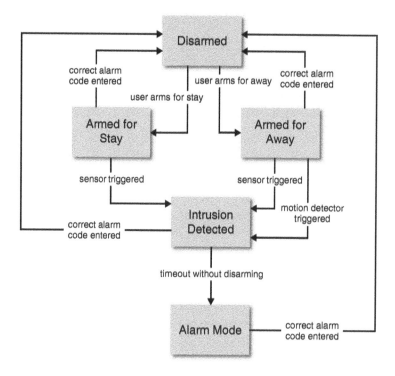

Figure 3.4 *A partial state-transition diagram that shows the behavior of a home security system.*

When Karl drew a state-transition diagram from that extensive event-response table he found some problems that weren't easy to spot by studying the table alone. There were missing events that should have led to a state change. One known system state could not be reached by any of the events listed. Other events didn't lead to the correct resultant state. Representing this information in two ways therefore revealed several requirements errors.

Event analysis also is a valuable testing aid. The information shown in both an event-response table and a state-transition diagram easily lets testers think of tests to determine whether the system behaves as intended. The tester can make sure that all possible events and transition paths have corresponding tests that will reveal any design or implementation errors. Getting an early start on testing with techniques like these helps the team build quality into the product from the earliest stages.

Related Practices

Practice #3. Define the solution's boundaries.

Practice #6. Understand what users need to do with the solution.

Practice #11. Create requirements models.

Practice #18. Review and test the requirements.

Next Steps

1. List the major events to which your product must respond. Classify them as business, signal, or temporal events.

2. Create an event-response table for the events from step #1. Confirm that your current set of requirements fully accounts for all the expected outcomes resulting from each event.

3. If appropriate for your system, draw a state-transition diagram to complement the event-response table. Look for any errors that are revealed by representing the knowledge in those two forms.

Practice #8   Assess data concepts and relationships.

The computing business used to be called "data processing" for a reason: All software applications create, consume, manipulate, or delete data. We can think of data as the glue that connects all the other requirement types; alternatively, functionality exists to process data. Both perspectives underscore the importance of exploring data considerations during requirements elicitation. Answers to the following questions help to define the solution's data requirements.

- What data does each component of the solution require? What are the sources of that data?

- What data does each component produce that should be retained?

- What stakeholders or systems consume each piece of data? How do they use it?

- What data objects are inputs from, or outputs to, entities that are external to the solution? By what mechanisms will data be received and sent out?

- What data objects flow between systems, components, or processes in the solution? By what mechanisms will the data objects be exchanged?

- What constraints, business rules, or dependencies apply to each data object?

- Which system or process "owns" each data object and therefore is the source of truth about it?

- What information needs to be input or displayed on a user interface screen?

- What policies must the system comply with regarding data governance, including quality, access, security, privacy, integrity, retention, archiving, and disposal?

Understanding Data Objects and Their Relationships

Data elicitation, analysis, and management are not small tasks. However, the BA needs to understand all the data objects in their problem and solution spaces to be able to specify the correct set of functional and nonfunctional requirements. To gain—and communicate—that understanding, the BA will create multiple views of the data over time and for different audiences. User representatives might be interested in a high-level view of all the data objects, shown in the form of a conceptual data model. Database architects will create a physical data model that defines how the database is structured. Developers and testers need the details that appear in a data dictionary.

Begin your data exploration by acquiring a full list of data objects: the logical representation of system information. Look for significant data objects in places like these.

- Pick out the nouns that appear in descriptions of the business problem, solution concept, processes, user requirements, state-transition diagrams, and event-response tables.

- The labels on the lines of an ecosystem map or on context diagram flows identify high-level data objects (see Practice #3, "Define the solution's boundaries").

- When stakeholders mention items such as a customer, order, or address, those likely refer to data objects needed in the solution.

- Descriptions of reports, displays, and other outputs give clues regarding data items the system must either receive as inputs or create.

- On existing products or when integrating with existing systems, the table names in relational databases likely belong to data objects. You may need to do some mapping or translation of data objects and terminology from one system to another.

After identifying likely data objects (*entities*), you can create a data model to show the logical connections between them (*relationships*). The *entity relationship diagram* or ERD is a popular convention for drawing data models (Wiegers and Beatty 2013). ERDs can represent conceptual, logical, or physical data views. A conceptual data model is sometimes called a *business data diagram* (Beatty and Chen 2012). Conceptual models identify only the business data objects and their relationships (Nalimov 2021). A logical model adds details about each entity's attributes. A physical data model describes the architecture of the implemented database, including tables, columns, primary and foreign keys, and referential integrity rules (ScienceDirect 2022).

A conceptual ERD for the restaurant online ordering project from Practice #3, "Define the solution's boundaries," might look like Figure 3.5. The entities appear in boxes. The lines show logical links between data objects, and the labels on the lines characterize each relationship.

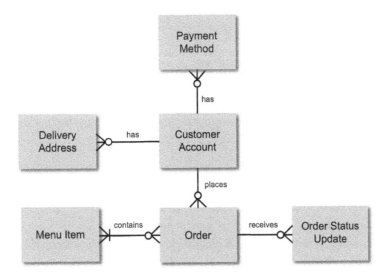

Figure 3.5 *An entity relationship diagram depicts all the data objects in a problem or solution space and their logical connections.*

The numerical nature of each entity pair's relationship—its *cardinality*—is shown on the line that connects the entities. There are several ERD notations available to show relationship cardinalities; this example illustrates the crow's foot notation (Abba 2022). Among others, possible cardinalities and their symbols include these:

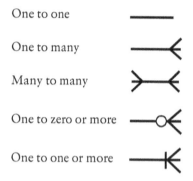

One to one	———
One to many	——<
Many to many	>——<
One to zero or more	——o<
One to one or more	——⊬<

In Figure 3.5, a customer account places zero or more orders, an order must contain one or more menu items, and a menu item can belong to zero or more orders. The BA could use this ERD during an elicitation review session to ask questions such as "Must an order always contain at least one item?" and "Under what conditions could a customer account have no delivery address?" Walk systematically through the data objects in the model to identify all their logical connections and verify the relationship cardinalities.

Refining the Data Understanding

Once you have the data objects in hand, look for functionality associated with them. A helpful acronym is *CRUD*: Determine how an instance of each data object is **C**reated, **R**ead, **U**pdated, or **D**eleted within the solution. Also look for ways that data objects are copied, listed, used, moved, and transformed, which leads to the much more amusing acronym *CRUDCLUMT*.

Make sure the necessary operations for each data object appear in process flows or use case descriptions. Look for data objects that are created but never used or stored, and for objects that are used by processes but are never explicitly read or created. Understand where each piece of data comes from and how the system inputs it. This analysis can reveal additional requirements about the data, possibly revealing more processes or use cases.

Data output requirements are important as well. Explore how the system will present data to users and send it to other systems or external devices. The system may need to perform translation, abstraction, computations, formatting, or other processing before presenting an output. Understand how the users will view the data in reports, interactive dashboards, or other extracts and how they'll want to manipulate the displayed data (Wiegers and Beatty 2013). These output requirements will reveal the functionality needed to build the output displays as well as some quality requirements, such as data latency and performance goals.

Ask your stakeholders about business rules, quality attributes, and other constraints that could affect your data objects but are not obvious from the data model alone. Although the ERD in Figure 3.5 shows that each customer account can have zero or more payment methods associated with it, through discussions you might discover a business rule stating that a customer account must have at least one payment method stored before placing an order. This business rule is not shown explicitly in the data model. Similarly, a security requirement could require that stored payment methods be encrypted, as they are personally identifiable information. Such constraints lead to derived functionality to comply with them.

To depict the movement of data through the system, consider drawing a *data flow diagram* (DFD). A DFD is a child of the context diagram, as though you took a magnifier and peered inside the single circle that represents the entire system in the context diagram. The DFD shows how data elements tie together the system processes that create, use, or change that data.

To create a DFD, show in rectangles the external entities that interact with your system. Those external entities also appeared on the context diagram. Circles identify processes that consume, transform, or produce data. Objects shown between two parallel lines are *data stores* that hold some chunk of data permanently, temporarily, or even only conceptually. Finally, labeled arrows, or *data flows*, between objects show both internal and external data inputs and outputs.

Figure 3.6 shows a portion of a DFD that builds on the context diagram from Figure 2.5. It's easy to walk through this model and see how the processes access, manipulate, display, and transform the various data objects. For instance, this model shows that process 3 lets the user build an order, process 4 transmits the order to the restaurant order placement system, and process 5 confirms receipt of the order. Make sure that each data object in your data flow diagram also appears in your ERD, as discrepancies between models reveal problems (see Practice #11, "Create requirements models").

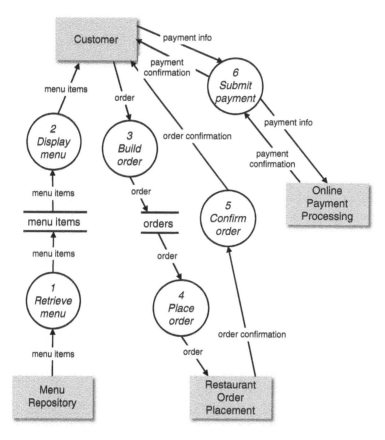

Figure 3.6 *A portion of a data flow diagram for the restaurant online ordering system shows how menu, order, and payment information is used in various processes.*

Data Details Determine Success

After you understand the data objects and their relationships, create a *data diction-ary* for each system in your solution. The ERD provides a high-level view of the data; the data dictionary supplies the details. Figure 3.7 shows a fragment of a data dic-tionary for two data objects from the restaurant online ordering site, Customer Account and Delivery Address. A data dictionary shows all the fields or attributes of each data object, along with various metadata about each field (Beatty and Chen 2012). Common metadata includes data type, length, business rules, valid values, whether a field is required, and whether a field must have unique values. Note that a data dictionary is not the same as a glossary of terms, abbreviations, and acronyms; see Practice #17, "Create a glossary."

ID	Data object	Field name	Description	Unique values?	Data type	Length	Reqd?
DD1	Customer Account	E-mail Address	The user's e-mail address. Also used as the user's login ID. A user must have exactly one e-mail address.	Y	Alphanumeric	Any	Y
DD2	Customer Account	Password	A combination of uppercase or lowercase characters and numbers created by the user. A user can have only one password associated with their login ID at a time.	N	Alphanumeric	6-12	Y
DD3	Customer Account	Name	Customer name for the account. Typically first and last but is treated as a single field.	N	Alphanumeric	100	Y
DD4	Customer Account	Phone Number	Customer phone number for order updates.	N	Alphanumeric	Any	N
DD5	Delivery Address	Address Line 1	First line of the delivery address.	N	Alphanumeric	50	N
DD6	Delivery Address	Address Line 2	Additional delivery address line. Used for apartment numbers, care-of instructions, and other optional information.	N	Alphanumeric	50	N
DD7	Delivery Address	City	City of the delivery address.	N	Alphanumeric	30	N
DD8	Delivery Address	State	US state of the delivery address. Currently, only the 48 continental US states are supported.	N	Enumeration	2	N
DD9	Delivery Address	Postal Code	Postal or ZIP code of the delivery address. Currently, only US ZIP codes are supported.	N	Numeric	9	N

Figure 3.7 *A partial data dictionary for the restaurant online ordering site shows the attributes of the Customer Account and Delivery Address data objects.*

Data dictionaries help align data requirements between systems. Carefully study the data types and field lengths for data items that systems exchange. Decide how to handle any type conversions and length mismatches. For example, if there is a length mismatch, determine whether the originating or receiving system should truncate the data or add pad characters to fit. If so, at which end should characters be cut or added? Such details can mean the difference between interfaces that work and those that cause data corruption or loss. Stephen Withall's book *Software Requirement Patterns* (2007) describes numerous patterns for precisely specifying a variety of data requirements to avoid overlooked issues that can cause errors.

If you're replacing an existing system with a new one, use your data dictionaries to ensure that data items being migrated from the old system to the new one match. Different stakeholders, systems, or interfaces might be using the same data field in different ways or using different fields to hold the same business data. In any of these scenarios, you might need additional logic for internal processes, data migrations, and inbound and outbound integrations.

The data dictionary ties in with elicitation of functional requirements, external interface requirements, and quality attributes. Although the restaurant we've been discussing serves only the United States today, perhaps the strategic plan calls for expansion into Canada. To enable that extensibility requirement, the team would need to extend the list of values for the state enumeration field, and they'd have to accept six-character alphanumeric entries for the postal code. Also, for each data object, understand if updates to the data must be captured in real time (transaction-based) or if a batch-based update is sufficient. A daily update is likely acceptable for your credit score but not for your bank account balance. Each decision will demand different processes and functionality to enable it.

Once external systems are sending data into your system, be wary of introducing new required fields, especially on agile projects where data interfaces are built incrementally. Each new field will demand changes to the systems sending in data, either mapping into the newly required field or defaulting its value.

Find Data Requirements Wherever They Are Hiding

Look for behind-the-scenes integrity and security requirements that impact your data objects. Your system's end users likely won't tell you about those types of requirements. You'll need to get them from other stakeholders, such as a corporate data governance group. Regulatory and legal standards, such as Sarbanes-Oxley Act compliance and laws relating to protection of personally identifiable information, dictate many data security, retention, and audit logging requirements.

Solution or database architects may specify requirements to support data access and performance goals. As an example, Karl's bank provides online access to monthly statements, but he must request statements older than two years from an offline archive. Obviously, the system includes some functionality to archive data periodically and to let users request and access older statements. No bank customer would ever present a requirement like this; they just want to see their statements.

Some people may see data requirements and data management as a technical activity best left to architects and engineers. However, the BA must understand the data objects in their problem space and the conceived solution, the relationships between those objects, and the corresponding data flows to be able to elicit the proper functional, quality, and external interface requirements. Without careful data elicitation and analysis, you may face—as Candase once did—fixing data length mismatches after the system's launch. It wasn't fun.

Related Practices

Practice #3. Define the solution's boundaries.

Practice #9. Elicit and evaluate quality attributes.

Practice #11. Create requirements models.

Next Steps

1. Create an entity relationship diagram for your solution if you don't have one already. Use it to assess your current set of data, functional, and quality requirements. If there are missing requirements to enforce or enable certain relationships, elicit the new requirements from your stakeholders and data models.

2. Create a data dictionary for your product. Analyze the incoming and outgoing data for data type, length, or business rule mismatches between what the system accepts or enforces and what the external systems expect.

3. Create data flow diagrams for selected portions of your system. Ensure that all data objects that appear in the data flow diagram are represented in the entity relationship diagram.

| Practice #9 | Elicit and evaluate quality attributes. |

When discussing their needs, users naturally emphasize the functionality they expect to find in the solution. However, we've all had the experience of using some application that contains the right functionality and yet we don't like it. Maybe it takes too long to perform a task, or the user interface is hard to figure out. It might crash frequently or have too many bugs. Perhaps as you use the software, it consumes more and more memory and eventually slows your computer to a crawl. Maybe those products satisfy their functional requirements, but they fall short of the user's (often unstated) quality expectations.

Solution requirements encompass both functional and nonfunctional requirements. When people say *nonfunctional requirements*, most frequently they're thinking of *quality attributes*, also known as *quality of service* requirements. These characteristics describe not what the product does, but rather how well it functions. If they don't explore quality attributes during requirements elicitation, the team might deliver a solution that doesn't please its users.

Product quality is a complex function of many characteristics. Also, quality means different things to different stakeholders. Expert users could value user interface efficiency most highly, whereas less experienced or only occasional users prefer a system that's easy to learn and remember. Maintenance staff are more concerned with maintainability and extensibility than with performance or efficiency. There's no single definition or measure of *quality*.

Some lists itemize more than fifty software quality attributes, using various classification schemes (e.g., ISO/IEC 2019, Wikipedia 2022). Table 3.5 lists several attributes that most software systems should explore during elicitation. Some of these pertain to external quality that users observe. The others are internal quality factors that are more important to developers, testers, and maintainers (Lauesen 2002, Wiegers and Beatty 2013).

Table 3.5 *Several external and internal software quality attributes*

External quality attributes	Internal quality attributes
Availability	Efficiency
Installability	Extensibility
Integrity	Maintainability
Interoperability	Modifiability
Performance	Portability
Reliability	Reusability
Robustness	Scalability
Safety	Verifiability
Security	
Usability	

Eliciting Quality Attributes

Exploring quality requirements is part of user requirements elicitation. Some users will spontaneously present their quality expectations. More often, the BA needs to stimulate the discussion by asking the right questions. Simply asking users "What are your availability requirements?" won't yield useful information. Their responses are likely to be vague, simplistic, and perhaps unachievable: "The system needs to be available whenever anyone wants to use it. Isn't that obvious?" To help the discussion participants think more carefully about specific availability issues, ask questions like the following.

- Is it more essential to have certain functions available than others? If so, which ones?

- What could be the downside if certain capabilities aren't available for a while? How could we best handle those situations?

- What time periods could be reserved for scheduled maintenance activities with the least adverse impact?

- Should the system notify users if some functionality is unavailable?

- How could we determine whether the availability goals were satisfied?

Roxanne Miller (2009) has compiled more than 2,000 questions a BA can use to elicit a deep understanding of fourteen important quality attributes. You won't need to ask 2,000 questions, but Miller's book is a valuable resource to help a BA elicit the right information about quality requirements from various stakeholders.

The first step is to identify those quality attributes that pertain to your product. Then, study compilations of questions relating to each of those attributes and select those that you think would probe around relevant issues (Miller 2009, Wiegers and Beatty 2013). This preparation will lead you to a set of questions that efficiently focus elicitation participants' attention on the significant quality characteristics.

Quality Attribute Implications

Unlike functional requirements, developers do not always implement quality attributes in code directly. Certain quality attributes drive architectural decisions, impose design or implementation constraints on developers, or serve as the origin of derived functional requirements. The BA needs to explore the various stakeholders' quality expectations and then translate those into clear, precise requirements statements to guide the developers' actions.

To illustrate the process of deriving functional requirements from a quality attribute statement, consider security. Perhaps your company's security policy contains this statement: "All information systems must require multifactor authentication before allowing a user to access system services." That concise statement leads to an explosion of questions like these:

- What types and combinations of authentication are acceptable: password, PIN, single-use access code, security questions, biometrics, or something else?

- For passwords, what are the rules regarding minimum and maximum password length, allowed characters, required and prohibited character patterns, and frequency of required password changes? Is the password case-sensitive?

What functionality is needed to let users create, change, and reset passwords? How will the system notify users when they must change a password, and let them do so?

- For access codes, how are they provided: text message, e-mail, phone call, or user choice? How many characters does the code contain? What are the allowed characters? How long is the code good for? What functionality is needed to let the user enter, maintain, and select phone numbers and e-mail addresses for these security checks?

- What happens if the authentication attempt fails? How much information should the system show in the error message? How many tries does the user get? Does the system lock out access after too many unsuccessful attempts? If so, how does the user regain access to a locked account?

And that's just for a single security requirement! The answers to those questions let the BA specify the detailed functional and data requirements to make it all happen. The key point is that simple statements such as "The system shall be secure" or "User identities must be authenticated" are woefully insufficient security requirements. They only provide a starting point for more thorough exploration.

It takes effort to elicit, analyze, and specify good quality attribute requirements. Some attributes, like this security example, provide excellent reuse possibilities across multiple applications. To get the maximum benefits from a good set of quality requirements, your organization would need to establish a mechanism for storing reusable requirements and nurture a culture that fosters reuse (Wiegers and Beatty 2013).

Quality Attribute Trade-offs

We have some bad news. Attractive though the concept might be, it's not possible to simultaneously optimize all the desired characteristics of any product. Increasing one attribute can enhance another, impair another, or have little correlation (Wiegers and Beatty 2013).

- Designing for greater robustness (how the system responds to unexpected operating conditions) increases integrity, reliability, security, and several other attributes.

- Enhancing security can require that users perform multiple actions to access an application, possibly using more than one device, which reduces usability.

- Increasing performance has little impact on installability, integrity, verifiability, and some other factors.

Because of these entanglements, it's important to understand which attributes are more important than others. That way, the decision makers can make the most appropriate trade-off choices. As usual with requirements prioritization, determine which quality attributes are most closely aligned with achieving the project's business objectives. That's not as obvious for quality attributes as it is with user or functional requirements. Practice #13, "Prioritize the requirements," describes a spreadsheet tool for performing pairwise comparisons of pertinent quality attributes to decide which ones will carry more weight when trade-off decisions are necessary.

Your stakeholders might not be thrilled to hear that their software cannot have the perfect mix of quality characteristics. A way to approach this conversation is to list the flaws the software might have: It won't be available 100 percent of the time, it might not be 100 percent secure, it can't provide an instantaneous response to every request, and so forth. Given that reality, and the constraints of finite time, budget, and skills, specify what level of imperfection in each of these categories the stakeholders are willing to live with. They still won't like it, but perhaps they'll understand the situation better.

Specifying Quality Attributes

Some quality attributes apply to specific functions, use cases, or user stories, such as the system's response time to a particular user action. Those can be documented as acceptance criteria for the requirement or story. Requirements experts Suzanne Robertson and James Robertson (2013) describe the use of *fit criteria*, quantitative and verifiable conditions the team can use to determine whether a particular functional or nonfunctional requirement has been fully satisfied.

However, other attributes have far-reaching implications for the entire product's design and implementation. Availability, efficiency, reliability, and scalability requirements lead to important architectural and design choices. They affect many functional areas and user stories. It can be expensive to correct shortcomings in these areas later in development.

Because of their broad impact, it doesn't work well to simply write down a presented quality attribute goal as a single requirement or product backlog item and throw it into the queue of pending work to be addressed at some future time. Instead, the BA needs to understand the various stakeholders' quality expectations and guide the developers' actions from the start. The Scaled Agile Framework (2021a) describes several strategies for handling nonfunctional requirements on agile projects.

One consideration on agile projects is when to evaluate certain quality attributes. On one project, Candase discovered that individual features or user stories didn't have specific performance requirements, but certain end-to-end processes within the system did. Deciding when to performance test and benchmark the results was tricky.

Set the benchmark too early in development, and performance would degrade over time as more complex logic was added. Test too late, and the team would lose the ability to address any performance shortcomings. Finding the balance was key.

As we saw, writing a fuzzy quality requirement like "The system shall be secure" doesn't help developers. A quality attribute specification should be

Precise (so people understand it),

Necessary (so you don't overengineer the product),

Measurable (so you know exactly what you're trying to achieve),

Verifiable (so you can tell if you've achieved it), and

Realistic (so you don't waste your time chasing unicorns).

One technique for writing precise nonfunctional requirements is called *Planguage* (Gilb 2005); see Practice #14, "Write requirements in consistent ways," for more about this keyword-oriented pattern. It's possible to write clear quality requirements even using unstructured natural language. Following are some examples; many others can be found in books by Lauesen (2002), Miller (2009), Robertson and Robertson (2013), and Wiegers and Beatty (2013).

Security: Files containing highly restricted data per the system's data classification must always be encrypted (symmetrically or asymmetrically) at rest.

Performance: The system's response time must be 1.5 seconds or less for at least 75 percent of user interface actions, and 4.0 seconds or less for at least 95 percent of user interface actions.

Interoperability: The application must work correctly with the most recent Chrome, Firefox, and Edge browser versions, as well as the previous three versions.

Verifiability: At least 90 percent of the system's functionality must be covered by one or more automated unit, integration, or functional tests.

Scalability: The system must be able to scale capacity automatically from four to six servers when incoming requests exceed 500 per minute.

Eliciting, analyzing, and specifying quality attributes is challenging. Nonetheless, the prudent BA will include this important dimension along with the other requirements development activities. If the requirements don't specify the users' expectations regarding important quality attributes, no one should be surprised if the product doesn't satisfy those expectations.

Related Practices

Practice #5. Identify empowered decision makers.

Practice #6. Understand what users need to do with the solution.

Practice #14. Write requirements in consistent ways.

Next Steps

1. If your team hasn't already done so, explore what quality means to your users and other stakeholders. Document that knowledge in forms that guide developers in achieving quality.

2. To better understand your product's quality characteristics, refer to books by Lauesen (2002), Miller (2009), Robertson and Robertson (2013), and Wiegers and Beatty (2013). Assemble a list of questions to use during discussions with your stakeholder representatives about quality attributes.

3. Confirm that each of your documented quality attribute requirements is verifiable and that someone has documented tests or other criteria that will demonstrate whether each is satisfied.

Chapter 4

Requirements Analysis

As the business analyst on your project, you've worked with key stakeholders to understand their objectives. You've interviewed user representatives and others to learn about the business domain, define the solution's boundaries, and identify stakeholder needs, expectations, and constraints. Now you must transform all that information into a description of the capabilities and characteristics of a solution that will satisfy those needs and expectations. That transformation process is the province of requirements analysis.

But what exactly does it mean to analyze requirements? A surprising number of books on software requirements don't even have an index entry for *requirements analysis*. Analysis sounds like something that just kind of happens through staring at requirements long enough. In reality, you can use several techniques to search for specific issues and produce better requirements—and hence better solutions. Consultant and author Eugenia Schmidt explains analysis nicely:

> Most analysts may elicit and capture the requirements through various means, but they may miss what BAs fear the most: overlooking something that is needed to build a valued solution. You can avoid that only by analyzing the requirements and the data. Classifying, sorting, prioritizing, visualizing, reviewing from different perspectives, finding conflicts, finding gaps—that's how we ensure that we provide the information that's needed to build or buy the "right fit" solution.

Requirements analysis involves ensuring that the needs of all stakeholders are understood and that a satisfactory solution to meet those needs can be defined, agreed upon, built, and tested. This chapter describes many tools to help the BA achieve this objective, but tools don't replace essential BA thought processes: questioning, learning, exploring, comparing, confirming, refining, and reassessing. The requirements analysis techniques are grouped into four practices:

Practice #10. Analyze requirements and requirement sets.

Practice #11. Create requirements models.

Practice #12. Create and evaluate prototypes.

Practice #13. Prioritize the requirements.

Practice #10	Analyze requirements and requirement sets.

Analyzing requirements is where a skilled BA really adds value. Whether it's performed explicitly by a BA or transiently in developers' heads, requirements analysis involves numerous activities:

- Partitioning a system into parts and determining how the parts relate to one another (Thayer and Dorfman 1997)

- Representing requirements knowledge at an appropriate level of detail and in suitable forms to ensure a thorough understanding

- Discovering and resolving conflicts, inconsistencies, redundancies, omissions, and dependencies

- Deriving detailed solution requirements from higher-level sources, such as system requirements, use cases, business rules, and quality attributes

- Assessing requirements for several quality characteristics

- Negotiating requirement priorities

Analysis is an incremental and iterative process. It begins when you have your first requirement. You acquire some information, evaluate and understand it, record it, and confirm its correctness. The first round ends when you understand some set of requirements well enough for the team to proceed with design and development at a low risk of having to perform excessive rework. Then you move on to the next chunk of requirements and repeat the process, keeping in mind that these sequential chunks could all tie together with potential conflicts and dependencies. As we saw in Figure 1.2, analysis is interwoven with ongoing elicitation, specification, and validation activities.

Analyzing Individual Requirements

Some analysis activities apply to individual requirements, others to sets of requirements. Figure 4.1 shows the major aspects of analyzing individual requirements. It's helpful to have a checklist of these items to remind you about the thought processes to go through. Just such a checklist is included in the supplementary materials available for downloading from the website associated with this book. As you gain experience, you'll internalize the list and know what to look for.

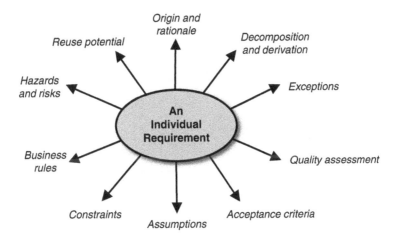

Figure 4.1 *Activities for analyzing individual requirements.*

Origin and rationale. You should be able to trace each requirement or user story back to its origin, which could be a stakeholder request, use case, policy, quality attribute, or some other source that led to including it. If anyone asks why a particular requirement is present, the BA should have a compelling answer. Understanding the rationale for including each requirement helps people make priority and scoping decisions based on the requirement's value to stakeholders.

Decomposition and derivation. A big portion of analysis is to decompose large or high-level requirements into enough detail that they are well understood. Finding the right level of granularity is tricky. There's no point in overly detailing requirements prematurely, particularly if they're likely to change or be dropped. However, you need a certain amount of information to assess each requirement's priority and feasibility, more detail to estimate their size and implementation cost, and still more to know exactly what to build.

Features can be decomposed into subfeatures or user stories and from there into functional requirements. A *feature tree* is an effective way to depict this decomposition visually, showing stakeholders a concise view of what they're getting (Beatty and Chen 2012). Figure 4.2 shows a partial feature tree for the restaurant online ordering site described in Chapter 2. Major, or L1, features appear in the boxes: Order Placement, Online Menu, User Accounts, and Online Order Payment. The lines coming off each L1 feature line point to L2 and then to L3 subfeatures. You might elect to implement various groups of subfeatures in different product releases, so the feature tree also is a helpful scoping tool, as described in Practice #19, "Establish and manage requirements baselines."

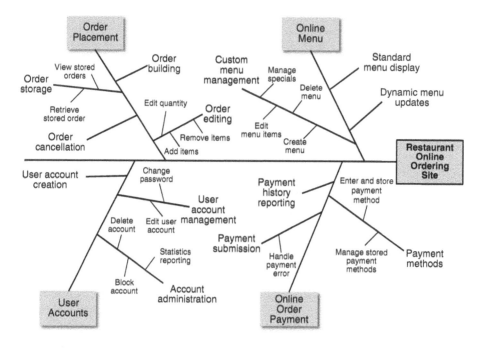

Figure 4.2 *A feature tree shows the major features and their subfeatures that make up a software solution.*

Agile projects may encounter user stories that are too large to implement in a single iteration, called *epics*. Epic splitting and story splitting are forms of decomposition that affect the workload planning in agile teams (Cohn 2012, Lawrence and Green 2022). Each resultant story should deliver some user value.

If you're employing use cases, analysis includes deriving functional requirements from the various use case elements shown in Figure 3.2. For instance, preconditions must be met before the system can begin executing the use case. But the preconditions don't tell the developer what to do if they *aren't* satisfied. It's better to have a

BA close those information gaps instead of expecting each developer to figure it out. The BA might derive additional functionality from quality attribute requirements or relevant business rules.

Exceptions. People naturally focus on describing how they expect the product to behave when everything goes well. However, developers write a lot of code to handle exceptions that could prevent successful execution. During analysis, identify potential error conditions—user actions, system conditions, or data values—that the system must detect and handle to minimize their adverse impacts.

Quality assessment. Experienced BAs automatically scan for certain characteristics as they review requirements. A statement that lacks any of the following properties demands further exploration and improvement (Wiegers and Beatty 2013).

- *Complete.* No necessary information is missing.
- *Correct.* The requirement accurately states a stakeholder's need or a necessary property of the solution.
- *Feasible.* The requirement can be implemented within known technical, business, and project constraints.
- *Necessary.* The statement documents something a stakeholder really needs.
- *Prioritized.* The requirement is ranked relative to others as to its importance and urgency of inclusion in the solution.
- *Unambiguous.* The statement conveys only one possible meaning to all readers. This is particularly important—and challenging—when team members have different native languages, where wording subtleties can cause confusion.
- *Verifiable.* There's some way to demonstrate that the requirement has been correctly implemented.

User stories should satisfy a similar list of quality characteristics, easily remembered with the acronym *INVEST* (Cohn 2004). Each story should be *I*ndependent of others, *N*egotiable during conversations with stakeholders, *V*aluable to customers, *E*stimable to assess size and implementation effort, *S*mall, and *T*estable.

Acceptance criteria. Consider how someone could judge whether the requirement was correctly implemented and ready for use (see Practice #18, "Review and test the requirements"). Acceptance criteria can describe system behaviors, tests, performance measurements, or anything else that shows that the requirement is satisfied. Agile teams typically document acceptance criteria to flesh out the details of user stories, including exceptions. That is, they derive acceptance criteria or tests rather than refining a story into detailed functional descriptions. Written in either form, it's the same knowledge because that's what developers need to know to do their jobs (Wiegers and Beatty, n.d.a).

Assumptions. An assumption is a statement that people regard as being true without definitive knowledge that it is true. People often make unstated assumptions regarding requirements. Conflicting and obsolete assumptions can cause problems later. One user might assume that a particular business process will be automated in the new system; someone else assumes that it will not. Try to make any requirements assumptions visible and validate them to convert those assumptions into facts.

Constraints. Constraints restrict the developer's design or implementation options. Common sources of solution constraints include business rules, compatibility with other systems, physical realities (such as size, interfaces, and materials), data and interface standards, and quality attributes. Project constraints include limits on budget, time, staff, and skills. Some requirements writers inadvertently impose constraints by including user interface or other implementation-specific language. Confirm whether those truly are restrictions ("It must be done like this for a good reason") or just solution ideas that someone proposed ("Here's an example of what I have in mind").

Business rules. Business rules often influence, or serve as the source of, specific pieces of functionality or data. It's important to know which business rules apply to which processes, functions, and data objects. See Practice #16, "Identify and document business rules."

Hazards and risks. Software-containing products that pose safety risks must include hazard analysis as part of their requirements analysis activities (Li and Duo 2014, Tran et al. 2022). Requirements analysis should also consider risks that could arise from each requirement, including these (Sommerville and Sawyer 1997):

- Performance impact on the system
- Security threats
- Business process impacts
- High complexity or novelty that could make the requirements hard to understand
- New development techniques or technologies needed
- Risks that specific requirements may pose to business strategies, enterprise architectures, legal and environmental factors, and the like
- Adverse interactions with other systems, components, or databases

Reuse potential. Requirements reuse involves both crafting requirements that can be reused in other contexts and finding existing functionality that your application could exploit. Consider both reuse aspects during requirements analysis. If a process or a set of requirements is likely to be repeated, consider creating a generalized template for those requirements to enhance reuse. Candase once had a project that involved multiple file-based vendor integrations. The transport of those files to the respective vendors was essentially identical; only the file locations and encryption keys would differ. The team created a template for the vendor integrations that every business area could use to insert their own vendor's name, location, and encryption key without having to replicate the functional requirements.

Analyzing Sets of Requirements

You can perform many analysis activities on individual requirements, but other aspects of analysis assess the relationships among requirements. Figure 4.3 shows analysis activities that a BA might perform on sets of requirements, such as those planned for implementation in a specific iteration or release.

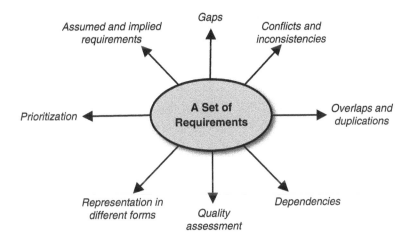

Figure 4.3 *Activities for analyzing sets of requirements.*

Gaps. When you examine a set of requirements, it's hard to see the ones that aren't there—they're invisible. Finding missing requirements involves reading between the lines. To assess completeness, trace downward from business objectives through user requirements and into solution requirements to ensure that they all align properly. Common sources of omissions include stakeholders who haven't provided input, missing exceptions, situations involving complex logic in which some combination was missed, and overlooked data. Requirements models provide a powerful tool for identifying gaps, as visual representation techniques make omissions far more obvious than textual representations can.

Conflicts and inconsistencies. Inconsistencies can arise between a parent requirement and its children. Requirements of the same type also can conflict. One says to do A and another says to do B, but it's logically impossible to do both. When developing iteratively, ensure that new requirement sets don't conflict with what has already been built without good reason and that new functionality won't break what is already there.

Overlaps and duplications. Look for multiple instances of the same information. Karl once reviewed several use cases that had nearly—but not exactly—the same data structure definition in three places. The reader doesn't know which one to believe, if any. Replicating information does make it easier for the reader, who sees the whole package of related information. However, replication raises the risk of generating an inconsistency if one instance is changed but others are not. When possible, point to a single, reliable source of the information rather than repeating it.

Dependencies. Some requirements depend on others being implemented at the same time or previously. For instance, it only makes sense to implement exception-handling code concurrently with the functionality where the error could occur. If you're enhancing a feature over time by gradually adding more capability, plan implementation so that each new subfeature builds on the previously laid foundation. A requirement also could depend on a certain feature being enabled or modified in a product to which it interfaces.

Quality assessment. Beyond the desirable characteristics of completeness and consistency discussed above, look for these other good properties in requirement groups.

- *Modifiable.* The collected requirements are organized and labeled in a way that makes it easy to change them and to keep records of the changes made.
- *Traceable.* It's possible to document logical links from requirements back to their origins, to related requirements, and to other development products like designs, code, and tests. Traceability depends on requirements having been written at a fine level of granularity and uniquely labeled.

Representation in different forms. There are many ways to depict requirements knowledge beyond natural-language text. Creating more than one representation using different thought processes lets you compare them to find problems. Excellent ways to find requirement problems are to create diagrams or tables to accompany the text and to build prototypes. Such alternative views of the requirements also facilitate clear communication with developers and other team members. See Practice #11, "Create requirements models," and Practice #12, "Create and evaluate prototypes."

Prioritization. No team can simultaneously implement everything in its backlog of pending work. Negotiating requirement priorities lets the decision makers sequence the work in a way that is technically sound and delivers the maximum, most timely customer value. See Practice #13, "Prioritize the requirements."

Assumed and implied requirements. Stakeholders sometimes assume that the solution will include certain functionality without them having to say so explicitly. Those assumptions can lead to disappointments; telepathy and clairvoyance are not effective requirements tools. The presence of certain functionality sometimes implies that other functionality is needed, again without explicitly calling it out. For example, an undo function implies a redo function. Decomposing a high-level requirement into a set of lower-level requirements to fully understand its complexity is one way to discover those implications and manage expectations.

Taking the time to carefully think about your requirements is well worth the investment. The potential rework you avoid by reducing requirements errors before they're cast into code easily pays for the time you spend on requirements analysis.

Related Practices

Practice #9. Elicit and evaluate quality attributes.

Practice #11. Create requirements models.

Practice #12. Create and evaluate prototypes.

Practice #13. Prioritize the requirements.

Practice #14. Write requirements in consistent ways.

Practice #16. Identify and document business rules.

Next Steps

1. Think about the requirements errors that your organization's projects encounter late in development or following release. What kinds of errors are most common? Consider whether more emphasis on requirements analysis could prevent any of those types of errors. Select techniques from this section that would help with analyzing your requirements.

2. Identify activities from Figures 4.1 and 4.3 that you have already internalized such that you simply perform them without consciously thinking about them. Create checklists of the practices that you don't perform automatically as reminders for when you analyze requirements.

Practice #11	Create requirements models.

Text is not the only way, and sometimes not the best way, to represent requirements knowledge. It's easy to get lost in a sea of details, missing the big picture and overlooking errors. Visual requirements models—diagrams—provide a great way to look at requirements information from different perspectives than the written solution requirements provide. Creating a robust set of requirements models allows the BA to iterate quickly on higher-level information, providing insights that lead to more accurate detailed requirements. Models can be updated easily as the product changes to reflect the current reality, which is especially valuable on iterative projects. Proficiency with requirements modeling is an essential BA skill (Wiegers, n.d.). Models aid requirements analysis in several ways.

- Models provide a context to see where each requirement fits in the overall problem or solution space.
- Violations of modeling rules can reveal omissions and errors.
- Models help the team discover missing requirements by ensuring that each element the solution introduces (process flows, system states, data objects, and so forth) has corresponding functionality defined to implement it.
- When multiple models that show different views of the same information do not agree, that conflict can reveal incorrect, missing, or unnecessary requirements.

Perhaps you've sat in a review session during which a BA presented hundreds of "system shall" statements line by line and then asked if their list was complete. We have; our eyes—and brains—quickly glazed over. We weren't useful in helping the BA determine if their requirements list was correct. Long lists of information are difficult for anyone to digest and evaluate.

Miller's Magic Number refers to how many pieces of information an average person can store and process in their short-term memory: 7±2 (McLeod 2009). Based on this concept, someone could examine five to ten discrete requirements and judge whether they were correct, complete, and consistent, but not hundreds. Requirements models help by chunking detailed requirements into objects at a higher level of abstraction in a diagram. A layered set of models lets people visualize information from the highest level of the solution boundaries down to the individual steps of a business process without being overwhelmed with complexity.

Additionally, people absorb information in various ways and wish to view it at different levels of detail. A developer needs the intricacies of every possible permutation of a use case, but an executive may only want an overall view of the project. A text-only view of the requirements might not communicate well to someone who learns best visually. For example, Candase has aphantasia, the inability to see pictures in her mind of objects that are not present (Dutta 2022). Therefore, asking her to visualize a process or a data flow from a natural-language description doesn't work. It isn't until she sees a graphic on paper or a screen that it becomes real to her.

Selecting the Right Models

Once you've decided that your team's work would benefit from modeling, you must choose the appropriate diagrams. Dozens are available for representing business processes, requirements, architectures, and designs. The various diagrams are collected in several modeling languages, including these:

- Business Process Model and Notation or BPMN (Freund and Rücker 2019)
- IDEF0 (Feldmann 1998)
- Requirements Modeling Language or RML (Beatty and Chen 2012)
- Structured analysis (Wiegers and Beatty 2013)
- Systems Modeling Language or SysML (Delligatti 2014)
- Unified Modeling Language or UML (Booch et al. 1999)

Rather than being a modeling language purist, use whichever diagrams will best convey the information you wish to communicate. Learn the symbols, syntax, and conventions for each model you decide to create. Avoid inventing your own notations unless you find that none of the available models will communicate what you're trying to show (which is unlikely).

Consider the characteristics of your project, what you're trying to learn and communicate, and your audiences when you select the models to create. When working closely with developers and testers, use low-level requirements models to depict the inner workings of the business or the proposed solution. If you're a BA giving a status update to the C-suite, choose high-level models that focus on objectives and scope. You don't have to model every aspect of your system. Create models that will enhance the team's understanding of those portions of the problem or its solution that are especially novel, complex, or risky.

Table 4.1 describes several models that are commonly used in requirements analysis. Many of these are illustrated elsewhere in this book:

- Root cause analysis diagram: Practice #1, "Understand the problem before converging on a solution."
- Business objectives model: Practice #2, "Define business objectives."
- Context diagram: Practice #3, "Define the solution's boundaries."
- Data dictionary: Practice #8, "Assess data concepts and relationships."
- Data flow diagram: Practice #8, "Assess data concepts and relationships."
- Decision table: Practice #16, "Identify and document business rules."
- Ecosystem map: Practice #3, "Define the solution's boundaries."
- Entity relationship diagram: Practice #8, "Assess data concepts and relationships."
- Feature tree: Practice #10, "Analyze requirements and requirement sets."
- State-transition diagram: Practice #7, "Identify events and responses."

Table 4.1 *Common models and their usage in requirements analysis*

Model	Description	How it helps in analysis
Data flow diagram (DFD)	A child diagram of the context diagram, the DFD illustrates the flows of data between external entities, transformational processes, and data stores.	Use this along with process flows to ensure that all processes that manipulate data are identified and have requirements to implement them. Use the DFD with the entity relationship diagram to ensure that all data depicted in the DFD appears in the data model.
Decision table and decision tree	Decision tables show every possible combination of conditions and the resultant outcomes. Decision trees show a series of sequenced decisions visually.	Use a decision table to ensure that you've covered all possible scenarios for a given set of decision data. Decision trees are easy to review with stakeholders for completeness and accuracy.
Entity relationship diagram (ERD)	ERDs can show conceptual, logical, or physical views of data in a system and the relationships between data objects.	The cardinality (numerical relationship) between pairs of data objects reveals the functionality needed to enable or enforce those relationships in the database. The BA can analyze the CRUD attributes of each data object to find missing requirements.
Feature tree	The feature tree shows the entire solution's feature scope in a fishbone shape. Related subfeatures are grouped in multiple levels.	Review each grouping of the lowest feature levels for completeness. Pairing with the requirements mapping matrix can unveil extraneous features as well.

Table 4.1 (continued)

Model	Description	How it helps in analysis
Process flow, flowchart, and activity diagram	A process flow shows the sequence of steps a business or a user takes to accomplish a task. They can be grouped into multiple levels to manage complex flows. Stakeholders can provide information for the diagram and review it for accuracy.	Analyze the lowest-level processes to ensure that each process step has associated functional and nonfunctional requirements and relates to a higher-level flow. Trace requirements to the process flow step they enable.
Requirements mapping matrix (RMM)	The RMM links multiple levels of related requirements data, from business objectives to features, to user requirements, to business rules, and so on. The RMM is similar to a requirements traceability matrix.	By examining each pair of levels in the RMM, the BA can ensure that all low-level requirements items link to higher-level data or model elements. A low-level item with no parent may be extraneous. A high-level object with no related children may indicate missing requirements.
State-transition diagram (STD) and state table	These models depict all possible states (statuses) of a data object's life cycle and the allowed transitions between them in either graphic or tabular form. They are also used to define the overall states a system can be in and the permitted state changes.	Use a state table to ensure that all of a data object's valid state transitions are included in the functional requirements. The BA can use a state-transition diagram with their stakeholders to identify errors and superfluous transitions that may complicate the object's workflow.

Using Models to Refine Understanding

Let's say your team is developing a new website for sales representatives to enter orders from customers who call in. You need to understand what activities the sales representatives will perform with the new site, so you start by creating a process flow. Process flows show the steps the user takes to perform a task in boxes and the decisions they make in diamonds—a flowchart notation. After discussing the order process with the sales reps who will use the system, you draw the diagram in Figure 4.4.

After you've created the initial model, walk through it with the appropriate stakeholders. Explain each diagram's intent, notations, and elements. This visual representation of their experience makes it easier for them to identify anything that's incorrect, missing, or obsolete. Use models to explore whether a process or a data structure could be simplified or made more efficient before the team builds a system to support it. You can also walk through tests to verify the correctness of your models, as we will see for this same example in Practice #18, "Review and test the requirements."

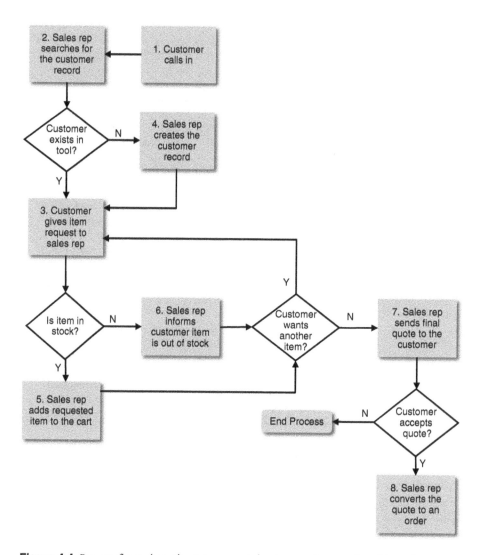

Figure 4.4 *Process flows show the steps a user takes to complete a task and branch points within the flow.*

During model reviews, probe for alternative flows and exception cases, as well as asking how accurately the model depicts a user's everyday job. For instance, when reviewing Figure 4.4, you might ask, "Can we revise the quote after sending it to the customer? If so, how does that change the process?" It's a lot easier to modify a model than to rewrite software when the users discover that something's missing or wrong.

As another example, suppose you're developing a billing system. You might draw a state-transition diagram like the one in Figure 4.5 to describe the life cycle of a single data object, in this case, an invoice for a construction job. Show the various possible statuses the invoice can have in the boxes. The arrows show the permitted transitions between various invoice statuses.

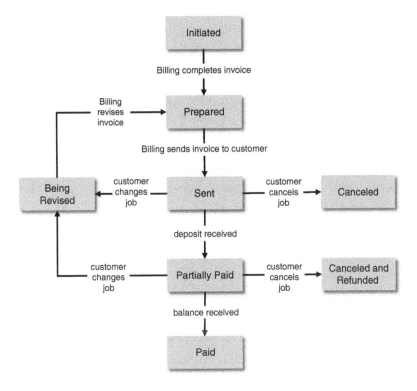

Figure 4.5 *A state-transition diagram that shows the life cycle of an invoice.*

As you walk through this diagram with your stakeholder, you might ask several questions.

- "Can an invoice ever go from Prepared to Canceled, or must we always send the bill first?"

- "Does the customer always pay a deposit, or could we go directly from Sent to Paid?"

- "Are there any situations in which the customer cancels a job but you don't refund the deposit?"

Such questions help you refine the model with a better understanding of the business. The answers could yield new requirements or identify unnecessary ones. Creating and evaluating models like these provides all participants with a common understanding of important aspects of business operations and solution behavior.

Iterative Modeling

Modeling is not a one-and-done activity. You will create, validate, review, and revise diagrams multiple times as you learn more and add new capabilities to the solution. Use tools that make this valuable iteration easier for you. During elicitation discussions, we like to use simple tools like whiteboards (both physical and virtual) and sticky notes. It's easier to move a sticky note around on a whiteboard than to redraw a box in a Microsoft Visio diagram. Once the model is stable, move it to a specialized software modeling tool to keep for updating and sharing (whiteboards and sticky notes don't travel well). Certain requirements management tools include some modeling capability. Dedicated diagramming tools like Visio and Lucidchart include the symbols and syntax for certain analysis models. Use whichever tool makes it easiest for you and your stakeholders to collaborate.

People have difficulty conjuring requirements—or anything else—from nothing. Draft, or strawman, models can be extremely useful to generate quick feedback from your stakeholders, especially early in the project. The beauty of strawman models is that they don't have to be accurate or complete to be useful. Just having something to study together helps stakeholders tell the BA what's wrong so that they can work together toward a more correct version of the model.

When utilizing strawman models, use a best guess estimate for numeric values instead of an X if you don't know the real value. On one project, a stakeholder hesitated to give Candase a dollar value for a business objective. On the strawman business objectives model, Candase supplied an outrageous goal: to increase revenue by eleven billion dollars. During the review, the stakeholder naturally said that eleven billion dollars was incorrect. That response opened a discussion about what the *real* number might be, thus getting closer to the correct business objective.

After creating a set of requirements models, compare them against one another. Having several representations of the same information allows the BA to look for discrepancies among them. Check that all the top-level features in your feature tree appear in the business objectives model and vice versa. Ensure that all functional requirements trace back to user requirements, business rules, or another source via a requirements mapping matrix. Trace functional requirements to individual model elements, such as steps in a process flow. Confirm that the data stores on your data flow diagram match up with entities in the data model. When models disagree, find out which one (if any!) is correct and adjust the others.

Requirements modeling is a powerful analysis tool. Having multiple people create alternative requirements views through different thought processes is an effective way to discover conflicting assumptions and ambiguities that would otherwise lead to incorrect conclusions—and the wrong solution.

Related Practices

Practice #2. Define business objectives.

Practice #3. Define the solution's boundaries.

Practice #8. Assess data concepts and relationships.

Practice #10. Analyze requirements and requirement sets.

Next Steps

1. Identify portions of your product that would benefit from enhanced exploration and clarity, and then select one or more requirements models that could yield the necessary insights.

2. Draft models for those types of diagrams that you identified as being informative. Review them with stakeholders to identify problems and then revise and finalize them.

3. Use the finalized requirements models from the previous step to assess your requirements set. Confirm that you've defined the requirements needed to implement all your processes, data objects, and state transitions. Update the requirements and models as needed so that they align.

Practice #12 Create and evaluate prototypes.

In an ideal world, a business analyst could simply ask users what they need and then record the answer in a requirements specification. In reality, a user is more likely to respond, "I can't tell you what I need, but I'll know it when I see it [IKIWISI]." The acronym *IKIWISI* acknowledges the challenge of exploring requirements only as a collection of concepts, text, and diagrams. As we saw with strawman models in Practice #11, "Create requirements models," people find it easier to critique something placed in front of them than to create and describe something brand new.

IKIWISI is the idea behind presenting users with prototypes and early releases of working software to give them an idea of what the solution could be and then refining it from that starting point. A prototype could be a partial, preliminary, or possible solution; a simulation of the ultimate solution as it's currently envisioned; or a demo or preview of an early version of a new product.

Prototypes can be used as elicitation, validation, and design aids. Prototypes make requirements tangible. Users can interact with a prototype, either physically or conceptually, to clarify and crystallize their true needs. Iteratively revising a possible solution lets participants agree on the solution's necessary capabilities and characteristics. Prototypes are a way to validate requirements that otherwise are recorded in diagrams and hard-to-visualize natural language. A prototype spans that fuzzy boundary between requirements and design, helping the evaluators transition from concepts to a physical reality.

The rush to deliver working code is not a substitute for exploring requirements using various elicitation and analysis techniques. You need some information about stakeholder expectations or marketplace opportunities to create even that first prototype. Also, iterating on code in an executable prototype or early product release is more expensive than iterating at higher levels of abstraction, such as concepts, models, and requirements (Wiegers 2022). Nor do prototypes replace requirements documentation. A user interface prototype only hints at the many details about functionality and data hidden behind the screens. Despite its limitations, prototyping is an excellent way to reduce the risk of building the wrong solution or trying to create a solution that isn't feasible.

Reasons to Prototype

If the requirements are well understood, the user interface design is routine, and you know the technologies are workable, don't bother with prototyping—just build the product. A prototype's value comes from using it to answer questions and resolve uncertainty. Agile teams create prototypes to "fail fast" by quickly learning what approaches or solutions don't work well, so they can adjust their strategy to better satisfy customer needs. You might create a prototype early in the project to decide whether to buy or build a solution. You could even take an existing off-the-shelf product for a test drive with your own data as a prototyping experience before buying it. Several kinds of prototypes can help you achieve these objectives (Wiegers and Beatty 2013).

An *interaction design prototype* offers users a visual representation that helps them assess whether a solution based on the current set of requirements would let them do their job efficiently. You can mock up some possible screens and ask users to imagine how they would interact with them to perform certain tasks. In contrast, a *technical design prototype* lets the development team explore under-the-hood issues before committing to a technical approach. The evaluation might reveal that certain requirements aren't feasible or cost-effective. Table 4.2 lists some reasons to create either of these two classes of prototypes.

Table 4.2 *Reasons to create two classes of prototypes*

Interaction design prototype	Technical design prototype
• Verify understanding of the business problem • Clarify poorly understood requirements • Validate a set of requirements • Discover previously unstated functionality • Improve business task flow • Reveal exception conditions to handle • Discover relevant business rules and assumptions • Reveal less-common scenarios • Gather feedback on visual design characteristics • Improve usability design	• Assess technical feasibility • Estimate potential performance • Evaluate a proposed architectural design, database schema, or core algorithms • Validate technology integrations and component interfaces • Judge implementation costs and risks • See whether a proposed approach could satisfy critical quality attribute requirements

An interaction design prototype can serve another useful purpose. Some new information systems either impose or accompany changes in an organization's business processes. It's hard for users who are accustomed to doing their jobs in a certain way to envision a whole new mode of working; some of them will resist the change. Too often, new system implementations simply repave existing cow paths, updating the interface while retaining outdated and inefficient processes. Significant process and application changes can push users out of their comfort zone. Those changes sometimes require additional training and alter, or even threaten, employees' jobs.

Influential user representatives who work with the software team to develop and evaluate prototypes can ease that uncomfortable transition. A BA, a user experience designer, and some users can explore ways that a system could support new business workflows. It's better to address potential points of user resistance during prototyping than after the new system goes live. This engagement also builds trust and buy-in from the user participants regarding the new future state, so they can lead others in the organization through the transition.

How to Prototype

View a prototype as an experiment. You begin with a hypothesis you wish to test or some questions to explore. The hypothesis could be that a set of requirements is correct and complete, that a particular user interface design approach will be well received, or that a proposed technical strategy is sound. Then you design an experiment to test that hypothesis, build one or more prototypes, collect information from prototype evaluations to either support or reject the hypothesis, and revise your approach accordingly.

Interaction design prototypes span a spectrum of complexity and sophistication (Coleman and Goodwin 2017). They can range from low to high fidelity, referring to the extent of detail and precision shown in the user interface (Robertson and Robertson 2013). Prototypes can be static, fully executable, or anything in between. Table 4.3 describes several interaction design prototyping approaches with varying degrees of complexity and realism. Dozens of software prototyping tools are available to accelerate the process (e.g., Capterra, n.d.).

Table 4.3 *Several classes of interaction design prototypes*

Prototype class	Description
Sketch	A simple, hand-drawn, low-fidelity drawing of a possible screen layout. Evaluators can visualize possible interactions without being distracted by screen design specifics. Also called a *paper prototype*.
Wireframe	A set of screen design layouts that tie an application's preliminary visual design to its information architecture. Can be drawn at low, mid, or high fidelity, often in monochrome to encourage evaluators to focus more on the screens' functionality than on their cosmetics (Hannah 2022).
Navigable wireframe	Wireframes of any fidelity level that incorporate navigation actions to let evaluators walk through the sequence of screens involved in performing a task. A way to animate use cases.
Model simulation	Some analysis modeling tools can simulate execution of a model by walking through the possible execution paths, employing user-specified logic and data to illustrate the model's behavior. No visual interface is involved.
Executable prototype	An implemented, interactive portion of the solution that appears to behave just like some part of the actual product would. Has a mid- or high-fidelity visual interface. Requires coding, real data, and operable interface functions.

Which sort of prototype to create depends on what you're trying to learn. Low-fidelity wireframes are adequate for requirements exploration. High-fidelity prototypes are best suited for refining detailed user interface designs. Prototypes that enable navigation between screens let evaluators simulate usage scenarios and help them refine and validate task flows and solution requirements. Executable prototypes are particularly valuable for usability design.

As an illustration, Figure 4.6 shows a pair of mid-fidelity wireframe prototypes for the View Article Statistics use case of the Speak-Out.biz publishing platform that was described in Practice #6, "Understand what users need to do with the solution." The left image is a high-level view of all articles and basic statistics for a mobile version of the site, while the right image shows more details if the author selected a single article to review.

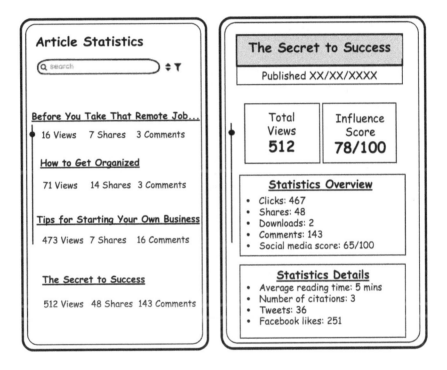

Figure 4.6 *Wireframes depict what the user interface could look like in order to analyze interactions and content.*

As you work with users to build and evaluate a prototype, keep these tips in mind.

- Engage the right participants based on what you're trying to learn. Choose people from the appropriate user classes, whether those are experts, novices, users of specific system functions, or other groups.

- Keep the prototype as simple as possible. It takes more effort to make a prototype look like a final product. The more polished the prototype looks, the more reluctant users and developers are to change it or discard it after it has fulfilled its purpose. A simple prototype is quicker to build, facilitates rapid iteration, and can answer many requirements questions.

- Resist the temptation or requests to keep adding pieces of functionality "just to see what it would look like" unless those additions enhance the prototype's informative value.

- Create scripts to direct users to perform specific activities or scenarios. Incorporate questions at strategic points in the scripts to elicit the information you need.

- Don't coach prototype evaluators about how to use the prototype. Let them work through performing a task to see how natural the workflow is, how quickly they learn to use an interface, how many errors they make, and how much they like (or hate) it.

- Don't be distracted by users or designers who want to fine-tune user interface cosmetics prematurely. That is, select the appropriate fidelity level to achieve your prototyping goals quickly.

- Use the evaluation feedback to refine the requirements. If necessary, use the new knowledge to create more prototype iterations to gain further insights.

The Prototype's Fate

After users have evaluated your prototype, you must decide what to do with it. A simple, static interaction design prototype obviously isn't useful in its current form. You retain the knowledge it revealed and discard the prototype. In fact, those are called *throwaway prototypes*. You can also harvest the insights from a technical design prototype, and then refine your planned technology approach to construct the solution.

Executable prototypes are trickier. They might look like a final product, but that doesn't mean they're usable. You probably implemented only the functionality that cried out for clarification. Prototypes aren't robust. They typically lack a well-done architecture and good implementation characteristics like input data validations and error handling, as just enough code was implemented to generate the desired user feedback. An executable prototype reveals little about the solution's quality characteristics: performance, efficiency, robustness, availability, reliability, maintainability, security, and portability. Managers or customers might pressure the development team to just finish up that nice-looking prototype and deliver it right away. However, a hasty implementation strategy could incur substantial technical debt that makes it harder to modify the system in the future.

The team should agree on their intent with an executable prototype at the outset. Will they use it as a learning tool and then build the real solution? Or will they use it as an initial product release and iteratively grow it into the solution? Communicate this intention clearly to all the prototyping participants, so the team doesn't prematurely release something with serious quality shortcomings.

Planned *evolutionary prototyping* is a reasonable way to build systems. Agile development, with its focus on getting useful functionality into users' hands quickly and using feedback to guide subsequent development, is similar to evolutionary prototyping. The key point is to build such a prototype or initial release with production-quality code from the outset. This minimizes the technical debt that the team will otherwise have to pay off later at a greater cost.

Related Practices

Practice #10. Analyze requirements and requirement sets.

Practice #11. Create requirements models.

Practice #18. Review and test the requirements.

Next Steps

1. Identify uncertain areas of your project's requirements that would benefit from prototyping. Craft a set of objectives like those in Table 4.2 that you'd like to explore further.

2. Decide which prototype classes from Table 4.3 would be most helpful in eliciting the information you need. Select some user representatives to provide input to and evaluate your prototype.

3. Build the prototype and have the evaluators work with it, using scripts and well-placed questions to elicit the requirements information you're looking for.

Practice #13   Prioritize the requirements.

A problem with requirements is that there are always more than the team can fit into the box bounded by time, budget, and resource limits. Even if you *could* implement all the requested functionality eventually, you can't do it all at once. To deliver the maximum business value in the shortest amount of time, you must decide which product capabilities to build first.

The Prioritization Challenge

Stakeholders might expect that they'll get some capability just because they presented it as a requirement. "Why would I have told you about it if I didn't need it?" they ask. Even though they're all called requirements, some are more required than others.

Prioritization considers how much each requirement contributes to achieving the project's business objectives. It lets the team determine which work items in the product backlog to defer or omit when necessary. Any prioritization process must consider the two dimensions of importance (how badly do we need it?) and urgency (how quickly do we need it?).

It's hard to get people to acknowledge that something they'd like to see in the solution isn't essential. They're afraid that they might never get some functionality they acknowledge as having low priority. Well, yes: That's the point. If you can't deliver everything, you want to make sure to deliver the most important items. To help stakeholders assess just how necessary a particular feature is, ask questions like these:

- What would you do if that feature weren't present?

- Is there a manual or automated workaround?

- Are there tasks you simply couldn't perform without that feature?

- What would be the cost or risk to the business if that feature weren't available in the first release? Or ever?

Prioritization begins when you discover your second requirement, because priorities are relative. It continues throughout the development cycle and even following release. As each new requirement or change request comes along, the team must evaluate it against the remaining work to know where to position it in the queue. As business objectives or competitive markets evolve, a feature that initially was planned for a later development cycle might float up in the priority backlog.

The term *requirement* here refers to whatever type of requirements-related objects your team works with. They could be individual functional requirements or groups of them; features or subfeatures; use cases or flows within a single use case; epics or user stories. Because prioritization is relative, it only makes sense to compare items at similar levels of granularity.

For instance, you might do a first-cut prioritization on a set of use cases, having learned just enough about each one to do that ranking. Then, as analysis progresses, you could assess the relative priorities of individual flows within each use case to select a suitable implementation sequence. You might never implement certain alternative flows if other capabilities are more important and needed more urgently.

Factors That Influence Priority

Prioritization is challenging because diverse stakeholders have different, often conflicting, interests. Prioritization easily becomes an emotionally charged debate. Everyone thinks their needs are the most important and most urgent, but those with the loudest voices shouldn't necessarily get what they demand. Certain stakeholders, such as representatives from favored user classes, carry more weight than others when it comes to choosing items to fit into a specific development cycle. The many reasons why one feature would have a higher implementation priority than another include these (Leffingwell 2011, Robertson and Robertson 2013, Wiegers and Beatty 2013, IIBA 2015):

- The customer or business value it would deliver

- Its contribution to the project's or development iteration's goals

- Who requested it

- Anticipated frequency of use

- The cost, time, and technical difficulty of implementing it

- Its time sensitivity (urgency, window of opportunity, compliance, contractual commitment) and the potential cost of delaying its implementation

- How likely it is to change

- Dependencies with other requirements that must be implemented together or in a particular sequence

- The technical or business risks that implementing, delaying, or omitting it could pose

- Whether it could reduce risk on future development activities or lay the foundation for future strategic value

- Its necessity for legal, regulatory, certification, or safety reasons

Another prioritization challenge is that it's hard to quantify what *value* means. It's usually hard to put a number or dollar amount on the benefit that each use case, user story, or feature would provide. Fortunately, prioritization is relative, not absolute. It's good enough to judge the relative value that one feature would provide versus another.

Prioritization Techniques

Project teams use many methods to prioritize requirements. Use the simplest possible scheme that works for your team. If a conversation and a handshake lead to an agreement, so much the better. Usually, though, you'll benefit from a more structured method. Prioritization involves four steps.

1. Identify the people who will make priority decisions (see Practice #5, "Identify empowered decision makers").

2. Agree upon the prioritization method(s) to use and the criteria to consider for candidate requirements.

3. Evaluate the candidates against those criteria.

4. Sequence the priorities within a set of requirements and allocate them to upcoming development increments.

Table 4.4 summarizes several prioritization techniques (Wiegers and Beatty 2013, IIBA 2015, Simplilearn 2022). Some, like rank ordering, work well with small numbers of items but are intractable with a large set. You need to choose a granularity level that makes any of these methods manageable. It's possible to prioritize twenty use cases or user stories against one another, but not hundreds of detailed requirements.

Table 4.4 *Some requirements prioritization techniques*

Technique	Description
Three-level scale	A classification of requirements into three priority categories:
	High: Both important and urgent (must be included in the next release)
	Medium: Important but not urgent (must be implemented but can wait until a later release)
	Low: Neither important nor urgent (nice to have but we could live without it)
MoSCoW	A four-level classification of requirements:
	Must: Must be satisfied for the solution to be considered a success
	Should: Should be included in the solution if possible but isn't mandatory for success
	Could: A desirable capability that should be implemented only if time and resources permit
	Won't: Out of scope at this time but could be included in a future release

Table 4.4 (continued)

Technique	Description
Pairwise comparison	Sequential comparisons of pairs of requirements to decide which one in each pair is more important. Repeat this on the whole requirements set to float the highest-priority items to the top of the list.
Rank ordering or stack ranking	Arrange all requirements in sequence from the most important on the top of the stack to the least important on the bottom. Only one item can sit at the top of the stack.
Kano model	Classify prospective features into four groups (Munagavalasa 2014):
	Basic features (must-haves): Needed for product viability and expected by the customer. Their absence leads to dissatisfaction.
	Linear features (satisfiers): Enrich the product's capabilities, leading to proportionally greater customer satisfaction.
	Exciters and delighters: Differentiating features that increase customer satisfaction when present but don't cause a satisfaction penalty if absent.
	Indifferent features: Have little impact on customer satisfaction.
Relative weighting	A spreadsheet-based analytical approach in which prioritization participants rate each feature on a scale from 1 to 9 in four categories, which can be weighted differently (Wiegers and Beatty 2013):
	• Benefit gained by including the feature
	• Penalty incurred if the feature is absent
	• Cost of implementing the feature
	• Risk associated with implementing the feature
	The spreadsheet then calculates a relative priority from the ratings. Sorting the list by calculated priority produces a rank-ordered, prioritized feature list.
	Another type of relative weighting is the Weighted Shortest Job First or WSJF method (Scaled Agile 2021b). This technique calculates the relative cost of delay of each feature (value, time criticality, and risk reduction or opportunity enablement) and divides that by the relative cost or size.
Criteria matrix	A spreadsheet-based analytical approach in which prioritization participants select the criteria that contribute to making priority decisions and weight those criteria as to their relative importance. Next, they rate each candidate requirement against each criterion on a numeric scale. The spreadsheet calculates each candidate requirement's score from the weighted ratings (Gottesdiener 2005, Robertson and Robertson 2013).

Pairwise Comparison for Prioritizing Quality Attributes

Evaluating every possible pair of requirements to judge which one is most important is impractical for more than a few dozen items. However, pairwise comparison works particularly well when assessing the relative importance of various quality attributes, as described in Practice #9, "Elicit and evaluate quality attributes." You only need to consider perhaps twelve to fifteen items, a manageable size. Consultant Jim Brosseau (2010) created a useful attribute prioritization spreadsheet tool, as illustrated in Figure 4.7 for the restaurant online ordering site described in Practice #3, "Define the solution's boundaries."

Attribute	Score	availability	efficiency	integrity	modifiability	performance	reliability	robustness	scalability	security	usability	verifiability
availability	4		<	^	<	<	^	^	<	^	^	^
efficiency	0			^	^	^	^	^	^	^	^	^
integrity	8				<	<	<	<	<	^	^	<
modifiability	1					^	^	^	^	^	^	^
performance	4						^	^	<	^	<	^
reliability	7							^	<	^	<	<
robustness	7								<	^	^	<
scalability	2									^	^	^
security	10										<	<
usability	7											<
verifiability	5											

Figure 4.7 *A sample quality attribute prioritization matrix for a restaurant online ordering site shows that security and integrity are the most important attributes.*

Beginning with Brosseau's spreadsheet (available from the website that accompanies this book), first decide which of the many quality attributes pertain to your product. Then, for each pair of attributes, indicate which one is more important to success. A less-than sign (<) in a cell indicates that the attribute at the left side of the row is more important; a caret (^) means the attribute at the top of the column is more important. The second column in the spreadsheet displays a score for each attribute. Alternatively, you could write the name of the "winning" attribute from each pair in the cell and then count how many times each attribute appears in the matrix. In Figure 4.7, security is the most important of the eleven attributes shown, with a score of 10; efficiency is the least important. You could use this spreadsheet tool to prioritize any small set of requirements using the pairwise comparison method, not only quality attributes.

Analytical Prioritization Methods

Most of the prioritization methods in Table 4.4 offer no guidance about *how* to judge the relative priorities of requirements. The exceptions are the analytical methods, relative weighting and criteria matrix. These methods invite participants to consider multiple dimensions that feed into their priority decisions and then evaluate the candidate requirements in those dimensions. This is a more objective approach that mimics the team's thought processes. The calculated priorities provide a starting point for discussions to agree on what functionality to implement in early development iterations. You can download spreadsheets for the relative weighting and criteria matrix prioritization methods from the website that accompanies this book.

Figure 4.8 illustrates a criteria matrix analysis for eight features that are proposed for a hypothetical product. Six criteria are considered in this sample analysis; use whatever criteria you find meaningful. Each criterion receives a relative importance weight; the weights should sum to 100. The prioritization team rates each feature against each criterion on a scale from 0 to 10. The spreadsheet then calculates the score for each feature by summing the weighted criterion ratings. Negative factors, such as the cost to implement and technical risk, are subtracted rather than added to get the final score. Based on this analysis, features 1 and 7 should have the highest implementation priority, with scores of 4.3 and 3.6, respectively. Features 5 and 8 have the lowest scores; they can wait, perhaps forever.

				Criteria			
Weights:	25	10	20	15	15	15	100
Features	Business Value	Who Requested	Usage Frequency	Cost to Implement	Technical Risk	Time Sensitivity	**Score**
Feature 1	10	4	7	4	2	6	4.3
Feature 2	5	4	7	2	2	5	3.2
Feature 3	7	8	4	5	5	10	3.4
Feature 4	4	5	3	3	1	5	2.3
Feature 5	4	4	2	6	3	5	1.2
Feature 6	6	8	6	4	8	8	2.9
Feature 7	5	8	10	3	7	7	3.6
Feature 8	2	3	3	3	3	7	1.6

Figure 4.8 *A criteria matrix prioritization analysis calculates a score for each candidate feature based on a set of weighted evaluation factors.*

To combine prioritization methods, you might start with a coarse-grained classification using the three-level scale or MoSCoW method. That will reveal the obvious, top-priority features (or user stories, or whatever) that must be in the initial release to make the application useful. Then, rank order or apply an analytical technique to differentiate the items in each group. As the team works its way down that priority list, they can be confident that they're delivering the most significant capabilities.

Some agile projects take the approach of releasing a stripped-down initial version of the product with just enough features to test the marketplace and generate user feedback as a learning mechanism. Sometimes called a *minimum viable product* (MVP), this technique lets you assess solution ideas, customer appeal, technical approaches, and alignment with business objectives at low cost (Agile Alliance 2022b, ProductPlan 2022). The knowledge gained lets the team determine future feature prioritization.

Aligning stakeholder expectations regarding prioritization is important. Whichever method the team selects, communicate the technique and the rationale behind it to the key stakeholders, including those at the executive level. Otherwise, they might be confused (and unhappy) when they don't see all the functionality they expect in the initial product.

Deciding which requirements you'll work on first and the implementation sequence for the others is among the most vital requirements practices. Dynamically prioritizing the items in your work backlog is a core component of building a roadmap that leads from requirements elicitation to solution delivery.

Related Practices

Practice #2. Define business objectives.

Practice #4. Identify and characterize stakeholders.

Practice #5. Identify empowered decision makers.

Practice #6. Understand what users need to do with the solution.

Practice #10. Analyze requirements and requirement sets.

Practice #19. Establish and manage requirements baselines.

Next Steps

1. Assess the requirements planned for your next iteration or release, using the criteria of importance and urgency. Does that analysis make you change the priorities of the requirements planned for that development cycle?

2. Review the list of factors that influence requirement priorities from earlier in this section. Identify those factors that contribute to your team's thought processes for making priority decisions and any other factors that aren't on that list. Build a customized list to use when your team performs priority analyses.

3. Select three prioritization techniques from Table 4.4 that might be suitable for your project. Try each of them on a sample set of requirements to see which feels the most efficient and effective for future use.

4. Use the analysis illustrated in Figure 4.7 to prioritize the quality attributes for your product.

Chapter 5

Requirements Specification

Human memories are imperfect and incomplete. They fade and distort over time, and other people can't access them. Consequently, a software team should record the information it accumulates about requirements to serve as a persistent group memory.

Some people don't like to bother writing down requirements or other project information. However, the cost of recording knowledge is small compared to the cost of acquiring that knowledge or reacquiring it in the future (Wiegers 2022). Thoughtfully selected and properly maintained documentation is a sensible investment to improve collaboration among project participants and to refresh memories over time. Documented requirements also help bring new team members up to speed when they join a project that's already underway.

The term *requirements specification* refers to both the recording of requirements knowledge and the resultant deliverables. Requirements specifications span wide variations in content, structure, form, detail, and formality.

- **Content** includes business requirements, system requirements, user requirements, both functional and nonfunctional solution requirements, data requirements, and all the other information that project participants need to do their jobs. Besides the requirements statements themselves, you might record a variety of metadata about them in the form of requirement attributes.

- Teams can **structure** their requirements in documents, spreadsheets, databases, requirements management tools, wikis, notecards, or arrays of sticky notes on a wall. Each structure has its pluses and minuses. Storage structures that are searchable are more valuable. You can aggregate this information into a single collection or partition it among multiple containers, depending on the project's size and complexity. Karl once worked with a company that was building a huge software product. They had a top-level system requirements specification with about 800 items, and 20 similarly sized software requirements specifications, one for each subproject. It would not have worked to store all that information in a single container.

- You can record information about requirements in many **forms**, each of which presents a single view of the requirements. Text is the most common representation form, but other options include diagrams, mathematical expressions, prototypes, and more. Certain forms convey specific types of information more concisely and effectively than others. However, no single requirements view tells you everything you need to know about the problem or its solution (Wiegers 2006).

- A requirements specification for a system whose implementation will be outsourced, or one for a safety-critical product having multiple software and hardware components, needs a lot of **detail**. Colocated and highly collaborative teams working on low-risk products can get away with less written detail, although they still must contend with the limitations of human memories.

- A specification written according to a well-structured template, with numerous slots to organize various types of information, is more **formal** than a wall plastered with sticky notes that are easily grouped and rearranged. Storing requirements in a database is the most formal and systematic approach. However, formality alone doesn't confirm that you've written and recorded *good* requirements or *the right* requirements.

This chapter describes four core requirements specification practices for recording different kinds of information. The goal of these practices is to keep all project participants informed and aligned toward their common objectives.

Practice #14. Write requirements in consistent ways.

Practice #15. Organize requirements in a structured fashion.

Practice #16. Identify and document business rules.

Practice #17. Create a glossary.

| Practice #14 | Write requirements in consistent ways. |

Whenever you see the phrase "writing requirements," please mentally convert that to "representing requirements knowledge." Natural-language text likely will always be the most popular way to record software requirements—it's how people normally communicate. However, there are many alternatives, including visual models (diagrams), tests, screen designs, prototypes, decision tables, and mathematical expressions. Even text can take numerous forms: narrative paragraphs, bullet lists, hierarchically numbered statements, tables, and structured lists that avoid repetitive text (Wiegers 2006).

Each technique has its advantages and limitations. The key is to choose a representation that will communicate a particular piece of information clearly, efficiently, and accurately. Ambiguity is such a common problem with requirements that every BA should master techniques for writing unambiguous requirement statements (Wiegers 2006). The overarching objective is always clear and effective communication. It's not purity of style or conformance to some standard or convention.

Consistently following some patterns and guidelines makes writing textual requirements easier. The author doesn't have to decide how to structure each one, perhaps resulting in a mishmash of styles. Readers know what information to expect in each requirement of a particular type. Following a pattern can help ensure that all the necessary information is there and makes it easier for readers to find what they need.

Some Common Requirement Patterns

Functional requirements traditionally use the keyword *shall* to state how the system should behave under certain conditions or a capability it will provide. Common patterns for such requirements include:

> The <*user class*> shall be able to <*do something*>.
>
> The system shall <*let the user class do something*>.
>
> When <*some conditions are true or something happens*> the system shall <*do something*>.

The first pattern focuses on what a user can do and the second and third on what the system does. Use whichever pattern—user action or system action—communicates each requirement most clearly. Here's a sample requirement, showing two alternative phrasings, either of which is fine:

> Security.Admin.1. The homeowner shall be able to change the security system's passcode.
> Security.Admin.1. The security system shall allow the homeowner to change the passcode.

There are several good practices to follow when writing requirements (Alexander and Stevens 2002, Wiegers 2006).

- Write in short, declarative sentences. Pages of long, narrative paragraphs that force each reader to glean individual requirements from all the verbiage invite confusion.

- Write in the active voice to make it clear which entity performs each action.

- Refer to specific user classes rather than to a generic "user."

- If there's any possibility of ambiguity, name the system in question ("security system") rather than simply saying "system."

- Tag each requirement with a unique identifier. Avoid bullet lists, as there's no good way to refer to a particular bullet item.

- Avoid combining multiple independent requirements with words like *and*, *not*, *or*, *but*, *except*, and *else*.

Some people object to the keyword *shall*. They protest that reading a long list of "The system shall..." statements is monotonous, it is not how people normally speak, the implication of what *shall* means is ambiguous, and so forth. However, it's best to stick to a single term, like *shall*, and use it consistently, particularly with functional requirements. Some requirements writers randomly use a mix of *shall* and near-synonyms: *must*, *will*, *may*, *should*, *can*, *could*, and others. That blend leads the reader to wonder if there are distinctions among them, such as the level of necessity or priority the words convey. Certain government standards do precisely specify when to use each such term. However, unless you're constrained to follow such a standard, sticking with *shall* to describe functional requirements is less confusing than using an assortment of similar verbs.

Agile project teams employ user stories to document desired system capabilities. A user story identifies who wants the capability, what capability they want, and why:

As a *<type of user>*, I want to *<perform some task>* so that I can *<achieve some goal>*.

Returning to the security system example, we could write this user story:

As a homeowner, I want to change my security system's passcode so that I can prevent the previous owner from entering my house.

Consistently following this pattern lets those who contribute user stories state the need and the rationale for it clearly. Ensure that the *<type of user>* in the story is a human user or user class that can have wants (unlike software systems or inanimate objects). Consider who really cares about the functionality being requested, especially if your product doesn't have direct users or a user interface. Keeping the users in focus, even when they are not obvious, allows the team to understand why they are building certain pieces of functionality and for whom.

When an agile team fleshes out a user story's details to prepare it for implementation, they typically write a set of acceptance criteria rather than a set of functional requirements. Some acceptance criteria are written as tests that follow a pattern called *Given–When–Then*, which is described in Practice #18, "Review and test the requirements."

Levels of Abstraction

The specification for a large, specialized authoring system included this requirement:

> The system shall respond to editing directives entered by voice.

This requirement was mixed in with hundreds of others, none apparently larger or smaller than the rest. However, this short statement conceals a great deal of complexity. In fact, it implies an entire speech-recognition subsystem. (This was before speech recognition was routinely built into computers and mobile devices.) We could restate that request as a user story, but it still doesn't reveal the underlying complexity:

> As an author, I want to enter editing directives by voice so that I can write more quickly.

If you're building a speech-recognition system from scratch, this one requirement is huge! Even if you're integrating with a third-party speech-recognition component, there's a lot of work to do. But it was still stated as just a single requirement.

By their nature, some requirements will be much larger than others, and different types of requirements describe information at various levels of abstraction. We can use two techniques to make requirement sets more understandable.

1. Group items together at a consistent level of abstraction or granularity.

2. Use requirement hierarchies to manage complexity in layers.

Figure 5.1 shows the relative levels of abstraction for several types of requirements objects. Functional requirements and acceptance criteria are at the lowest abstraction level or, alternatively, the finest granularity. Each one describes an individual bit of system behavior, from the perspective of either what to build (requirement) or how to tell if what you built is working as intended (acceptance criterion). User stories lie at a higher abstraction level; each story could have multiple acceptance criteria. Use cases are at a still higher level. It takes multiple functional requirements or user stories to specify the full richness of a use case.

Figure 5.1 *Relative abstraction levels for several types of requirements objects.*

Product features are the next rung on the abstraction ladder. A feature typically encompasses multiple use cases or stories, each describing something a user could do with elements of that feature. Finally, agile projects describe an *epic* as a complete user workflow or large body of work that comprises multiple user stories and can encompass several product features (Adams, n.d.). An epic might begin as a particularly large user story that must be split into a set of smaller stories to plan its incremental implementation.

During requirements discussions, the BA should remain aware of these abstraction levels. Sometimes a user will describe some functionality that the BA recognizes as being just a portion of a use case, feature, or epic that calls for further exploration. In other cases, as with the "editing directives entered by voice" example, the BA realizes that a presented requirement is a much bigger request that must be broken down further for understanding and planning.

To manage the complexity, avoid mixing high-level and detailed requirements items as if they're all the same type of thing. Requirements development involves the progressive refinement of details. Start with just enough information about epics, features, or use cases to allow relative prioritization and further analysis. Then, flesh out the specifics before implementation so that the project participants have a clear understanding of what to build and how it should function. Decompose high-level objects into similar levels of granularity—individual pieces of functionality—to understand their impacts, more accurately estimate the effort needed to build them, and plan an implementation sequence. Alternatively, you can aggregate detailed requirements into higher-level groups for easier digestibility. Hierarchically structuring requirements specifications lets readers get the level of understanding they need at any given time.

Requirement Attributes

A requirement statement describes some desired stakeholder need or solution functionality, but that's just a starting point. To fully understand the requirement, you should specify several additional attributes. Attributes that will meet most projects' needs include these (Alexander and Stevens 2002, Robertson and Robertson 2013, Wiegers and Beatty 2013):

- ID (How is this requirement identified with a unique and persistent label and/ or name?)

- Author (Who wrote the requirement?)

- Origin or source (Who requested the requirement, or did it arise from a business rule, use case, or some other piece of information?)

- Rationale (Why is it included? What's the stakeholder's goal or the business justification?)

- Priority (How important is the capability, how urgently is it needed compared to others, and why?)

- Status (How is the requirement proceeding through its life cycle from being drafted to approved—or rejected—and then implemented, verified, deferred, or deleted?)

- Validation method (How will we ensure that it's a correct and necessary requirement that will satisfy a stakeholder's need?)

- Acceptance criteria (How can we determine whether the requirement was correctly implemented?)

- Version history (How has the requirement evolved over time?)

- Estimate (How much work will it take to implement the requirement?)

- Dependencies (What other functionality or preconditions must be in place for this requirement to work correctly?)

Don't get carried away when choosing which requirement attributes to record. Start with a minimal set, not with a long list that people simply won't populate or use. Add more when the team will benefit from them.

It's relatively easy to manage a suite of requirement attributes when they're stored in a spreadsheet, database, or requirements management tool. It's clumsier—and bulkier—when requirements reside in a document, on index cards, or on sticky notes. Choose a storage structure that will accommodate the attributes you decide are important, as described in Practice #15, "Organize requirements in a structured fashion."

Nonfunctional Requirements

Quality attributes and other nonfunctional requirements also can be specified using structured patterns. Certain patterns let you specify desired quality characteristics more precisely than is possible using fuzzy natural language. One such technique is called *Planguage*, which is derived from "plan" and "language." Developed by Tom Gilb, Planguage provides an extensive set of keywords that invite careful thinking of just what's desired and ways to express those desires exactly (Simmons 2001, Gilb 2005, Wiegers and Beatty, n.d.b). Table 5.1 lists the core Planguage keywords needed for specifying quality attributes, using an availability goal to illustrate.

Table 5.1 *Core Planguage keywords for defining quality attribute requirements*

Keyword	Meaning
Tag	A unique label for the requirement, expressed hierarchically: "Availability.MaintenanceDowntime."
Ambition	A textual description of the intent for the requirement: "Perform scheduled system maintenance and install upgrades in a way that minimizes the impact on users affected by the downtime."
Scale	The measurement method that quantifies the requirement: "Minutes between when the system goes offline and when full functionality is restored."
Meter	How the measurement is performed: "Readings from the host computer's system clock upon going offline and access being restored."
Goal	A committed target value that will satisfy the requirement: "Average of no more than 1 hour per week."
Stretch	A more aggressive target value that achieves greater stakeholder satisfaction: "Average of no more than 1.5 hours per month."
Wish	A target value that reflects the stakeholder's desire in an ideal, yet realistic, world: "Maximum of 4 hours per year."

It takes more thought and more space to write quality attribute requirements using Planguage than to write a simple—if unrealistic—statement like "The system shall be available 24/7." For products that demand especially thorough and rigorous specification, Stephen Withall (2007) describes many patterns for precisely specifying functional, data, and quality requirements.

Recording requirements in consistent styles makes it easier both for the writer to structure the information and for the reader to access and apply it. As always, anything that facilitates effective requirements communication is good; anything that inhibits it is evil.

Related Practices

Practice #9. Elicit and evaluate quality attributes.

Practice #15. Organize requirements in a structured fashion.

Next Steps

1. Examine the list of possible requirement attributes in this section to select an initial set that would provide value to your team and that team members would populate and use.

2. Review some of your recent requirements to see if they're written in a consistent style according to clearly understandable patterns and specified at a similar level of granularity. If not, make appropriate adjustments to make the requirements as easy as possible to understand.

3. Review your set of requirements to see if they are structured hierarchically to manage the complexity of large requirements. If not, consider whether organizing them hierarchically would make the requirements easier to work with and manage.

4. Try writing one or two quality attribute requirements using the Planguage keyword template.

Practice #15   Organize requirements in a structured fashion.

Every sizable software project accumulates an extensive set of requirements information. Functional requirements make up the majority on a traditional project. An agile project team creates a set of user stories that represent explanations of user objectives, solution features, and desired functionality. All projects also have information about user classes and other stakeholders, business objectives, quality attributes, constraints, assumptions, business rules, and more.

The subdomain of requirements specification addresses how to record and organize all this information so that project participants can use it to guide their work. An organized knowledge collection facilitates effective communication and collaboration among the team members, particularly when they aren't all colocated.

Requirements Templates

If you're recording requirements in documents, adopt standard templates that your organization finds effective. If you work on different classes of projects—large and small, developed in-house and outsourced, low risk and high risk—create a family of templates so that each team can select the most suitable one for its project.

Figure 1.1 identified three documents—or more accurately, containers—to hold various groups of requirements information:

- Vision and scope document, for business requirements (see Figure 2.2 for a template)
- User requirements document
- Software requirements specification, for solution requirements

These containers hold different information, although a smaller project can certainly combine them into a single deliverable. As mentioned in this chapter's introduction, these containers can take on various physical forms. We'll call those containers *documents* here for convenience. Regardless of how you choose to store it, every project needs to collect and manage the kinds of information that appear in templates for those documents.

Thoughtfully selected templates provide several benefits. The template sections provide slots to hold various pieces of information. Organize those sections to benefit the people who must access the information rather than for the convenience of whoever writes it. Templates also let members of the development team know where to find the information they need.

One challenge of any requirements process is identifying the holes where information is missing. A well-structured template serves as a checklist, a reminder to avoid overlooking some topic. The BA populates sections of the template as they encounter information during requirements development, not from top to bottom. As time goes on, the BA might notice that some section—perhaps "Limitations and Exclusions" in the vision and scope document—is empty. This raises some questions. Are there any limitations or exclusions? Has the BA not yet had the conversations they should have with some people to explore that issue? Did they put information about limitations and exclusions somewhere else? If there's nothing to say about a topic, leave the section in place but insert a comment like "No limitations or exclusions have been identified" so that the reader knows it wasn't simply overlooked.

A good template is comprehensive, suitable for use on many projects. Use a "shrink-to-fit" philosophy when adapting templates to meet each project's needs (Wiegers 2022). Tailor your templates as needed with modifications such as these:

- Revise the terminology to reflect your project, culture, or audience
- Consolidate template sections to simplify the structure if that won't cause confusion

- Rearrange the template sections so that the deliverable makes the most sense for its readers

- Combine some documents or split the template into multiple documents if that helps to manage size, complexity, communication, or document storage, access, and revision

The idea of a template is valuable even if you're storing requirements in some structure other than word processing documents. Choose the various categories of information so that you can both organize input as it arrives and notice when the team has not yet addressed some topic. Use headings to group common information together. Distinguishing functionality descriptions from nonfunctional requirements, business requirements, data definitions, and all the rest is a useful organizational aid. An unorganized collection with diverse requirements information all mixed together isn't a requirements specification. It's just a pile of thoughts.

The Software Requirements Specification

The traditional core deliverable from requirements development is a *software requirements specification* or SRS. The SRS serves as the primary container for both functional and nonfunctional requirements that describe the solution's capabilities and characteristics. Different organizations call this deliverable by various names, including business requirements document or BRD, functional specification, and simply requirements document. Because of the confusion around requirements terminology, each organization should use deliverable names consistently and define their contents and purpose, so everyone knows what to expect to find in each one.

Figure 5.2 shows a typical SRS template, which you may download from the website that accompanies this book (Wiegers and Beatty 2013). You can find many similar templates in various requirements books or online. This template includes sections for many types of requirements-related information. Some of your projects might not need all these sections, but beginning with a comprehensive template lets you consider which of these categories do pertain to your situation. That's better than overlooking something important just because you didn't think of it.

Section 3 from Figure 5.2, System Features, normally will be the largest section of any document created using this template. That's where you'll find the functional requirements that developers are to implement. Organize the functional requirements in whatever way makes sense for your development team. You could group them by feature as shown here, or by use case, event and response, user class, subsystem, functional area, object class, or any other logical grouping.

1. **Introduction**
    1.1   Document Purpose
    1.2   Document Conventions
    1.3   Project Scope
    1.4   References
2. **Overall Description**
    2.1   Product Perspective
    2.2   User Classes and Characteristics
    2.3   Operating Environment
    2.4   Design and Implementation Constraints
    2.5   Assumptions and Dependencies
3. **System Features**
    3.x   System Feature X
         3.x.1   Description
         3.x.2   Functional Requirements
4. **Data Requirements**
    4.1   Logical Data Model
    4.2   Data Dictionary
    4.3   Reports
    4.4   Data Integrity, Retention, and Disposal
5. **External Interface Requirements**
    5.1   User Interfaces
    5.2   Software Interfaces
    5.3   Hardware Interfaces
    5.4   Communications Interfaces
6. **Quality Attributes**
    6.1   Usability
    6.2   Performance
    6.3   Security
    6.4   Safety
    6.x   [others]
7. **Internationalization and Localization Requirements**
8. **Other Requirements**
9. **Glossary**
10. **Analysis Models**

Figure 5.2 *A rich software requirements specification template (adapted from* Software Requirements, 3rd Edition *by Karl Wiegers and Joy Beatty).*

Some projects may produce additional requirements deliverables. As Practice #2, "Define business objectives," described, a vision and scope document contains the business requirements that set the stage for the rest of the project work. A complex systems development project will start with an overall system requirements specification or SyRS that describes the top-level product behaviors (ISO/IEC/IEEE 2018). From the SyRS, a requirements engineer might write multiple software and hardware requirements specifications to describe the subsystems that make up the entire product. Government organizations often create a concept of operations or CONOPS document, which serves as a user (or stakeholder) requirements specification. But the common deliverable that pertains to all software projects is the SRS. Remember, this need not be a traditional document; it's a container for the information that specifies the solution's details.

The various structures in which you can store requirements—documents, spreadsheets, requirements management tools, wikis, notecards, or something else—all have their advantages and their limitations. Whichever method you select should have several properties.

- Readers should understand how the requirements are organized, where to find what they're looking for, and how to use the collection. Include a brief description to this effect, as in section 1.2, Document Conventions, in the template in Figure 5.2. A table of contents also is helpful.

- The storage format should be easy to modify as requirements come, go, and evolve.

- Users should be able to search for the information they seek.

- Individual requirements need unique, persistent identifiers so that people can refer to them and link them to other project elements like tests. A hierarchical numbering scheme is fragile because a requirement's identifier can change when other requirements are inserted or deleted above it. Identifiers based on a hierarchical labeling scheme—such as Password.Temporary.Request—can be unique, persistent, and meaningful.

- The structure should let you define various requirement attributes that provide a richer understanding of each item, as described in Practice #14, "Write requirements in consistent ways."

Requirements Management Tools

An effective alternative to requirements documents is to store the information in a database. Dozens of requirements management (RM) tools are available for this purpose (Smith 2023). They range from simple, open source products available for free download to complex commercial packages that can handle huge systems development projects. These tools make it much easier to work with requirements than documents or other representations permit. They may provide the ability to do the following:

- Define a requirements classification schema so that you can store distinct kinds of requirements separately with their own user-defined attributes. This schema echoes the headings found in a document template.

- Track versions of individual requirements and their implementation status as they change over time.

- Define traceability links between pairs of requirements objects and sometimes to other objects stored elsewhere, such as models, design elements, code modules, tests, and project tasks.

- Report which requirements could be affected if a particular one is modified.

- Generate reports that extract subsets of requirements according to user-specified criteria and format the results to look like an SRS.

- Define baselines for specific development increments by selecting a specific subset of requirements from the database.

- Facilitate reusing requirements in multiple projects.

Don't expect that simply buying an RM tool will solve all your requirements problems. Converting from your previous requirements structure to using a tool involves both a technical and a cultural transition (Wiegers and Beatty 2013). The team will need to learn how to make the tool work for them: when to enter information into the tool; who can create, modify, and access the contents; get into the habit of using the tool as the authoritative requirements repository; keep the contents current; and so forth.

Remember that these are requirements *management* tools, not requirements *development* tools. They won't help you identify your stakeholders, ask the right elicitation questions, write error-free requirements, or find missing requirements. Invest in an RM tool only after the team has confidence in those fundamental business analysis skills.

When you're initiating a new project, take some time to think about the most effective and efficient way to organize, store, and communicate your requirements information. Decide what details to record about each type of requirement. All project participants should be able to readily find the information they need and update it when necessary. This will help keep everyone working from the same solution description toward a successful outcome.

Related Practices

Practice #14. Write requirements in consistent ways.

Practice #16. Identify and document business rules.

Next Steps

1. Compare your project's requirements set with the SRS template in Figure 5.2. Identify any categories of information that you're not currently collecting and storing. If your project team would find the information in those categories valuable, modify your storage—and perhaps elicitation—processes to include them.

2. Assess the benefits and limitations of your current requirements storage mechanism. Can everyone quickly locate the information they need? Is the repository updated when things change so that everyone always knows what the current requirements are? If you discover any issues with your current approach, modify it to reduce inefficiencies and avoid potential errors in the future.

Practice #16   Identify and document business rules.

Karl's friend Jeremy visited his local blood bank's website and made an appointment to donate blood later that day. However, when Jeremy arrived at the blood bank, the staff told him that they didn't take same-day appointments, even though the website let him make such an appointment. He was annoyed.

Jeremy's experience illustrates the problems that can arise when software fails to properly enforce or comply with established rules. The blood bank had a policy—no same-day appointments—but the appointment website's designer didn't make the software comply with the policy. Therefore, it had to be enforced manually (and inconveniently) by the blood bank staff.

This policy is an excellent example of a *business rule*. It's not a software requirement, as it applies to manual operations too. If Jeremy had called the blood bank to make an appointment for later in the day, some staff member would have told him, "Sorry, we can't make same-day appointments." The policy should have served as the origin of functional requirements for the blood bank's appointment system. Everyone needs to know about the relevant business rules and must interpret and apply them in the same way. In this case, someone dropped the ball.

Business Rules Defined

Business rules—or business logic—are statements that define or restrict certain aspects of an organization's operations or influence the behaviors of people and software systems within the organization. As with Jeremy's case, business rules often exist and apply beyond the scope of any particular software application.

The idea of a business rule goes far beyond the obvious domain of corporate business operations and their associated information systems. All enterprises operate under business rules, although perhaps by other names. Even games have rules regarding what actions the players and characters may and may not perform.

Business rules can be classified in several ways (von Halle 2002). Table 5.2 defines several common rule categories. Many rules impose constraints on how the business operates, including on data values and relationships, which can influence database design.

Table 5.2 *Common categories of business rules*

Rule type	Description
Term	A definition of a business concept.
Fact	A statement that is true about the business.
Constraint	A statement that restricts the behaviors of people who work in the business. Constraints limit, prohibit, or require some action.
Action Enabler	A statement of conditions or events that trigger some activity.
Inference	A new piece of knowledge or rule that's derived from other pieces of information or rules.
Computation	A statement or mathematical formula that defines how to perform some calculation.

You can write business rules according to various patterns, depending on what type of rule it is. Constraints often follow this pattern (Morgan 2002):

<subject> must [or may not or may only] *<constraint>*.

A retail store might have these refund policies for customer returns:

RET-1. A customer must present a receipt to obtain a refund on a returned product.

RET-2. Only store credit may be issued for products purchased more than 30 days prior to being returned.

RET-3. Refunds may not be issued for products purchased more than 90 days prior to being returned.

Action-enabling business rules may follow this pattern:

If *<something happens or some condition exists>* then *<perform some action>*.

Here's an action enabler for an online store:

RET-4. If the return shipping cost exceeds the price of a defective product being returned for a refund, then notify the customer that they don't need to return the product.

Every rule should have a unique identifier so that people can refer to it unambiguously rather than duplicating the rule wherever it applies. Pointing to the master instance of the rule instead of copying it eliminates the possibility of generating inconsistencies. The pointer approach also automatically updates all affected requirements if a rule is updated.

Record and maintain business rules separately from project-specific documentation. When rules apply to the organization as a whole, consider them to be an enterprise-level asset. This also facilitates reusing the rules in a consistent way across multiple software systems that they affect.

Discovering Business Rules

Every organization operates under a set of policies or rules, but they aren't always documented in accessible forms. Sometimes the policies are woven into the organization's historical culture, like tribal folklore around the campfire. You might be able to pull business rules out of existing systems. They're often discovered buried in code through reverse engineering on a software archaeology expedition. However, people shouldn't have to extract an organization's core business logic from application code.

Common collected sources of business rules include corporate policies (such as security policies), laws, regulations, glossaries, data catalogs, and industry standards. Regulated industries such as banking, healthcare, and insurance have many rules codified in applicable regulations or company policies. Government agencies are subject to countless business rules. These can become highly complex and interact in ways that require careful implementation in software. Interface standards such as networking protocols can be considered business rules as well.

During requirements elicitation, the BA should actively look—and listen—for places where relevant business rules might lurk. Sometimes the team knows about the rules already, as when domain subject matter experts work with the BA. In other cases, you can spot places where it seems that rules might apply and then probe those further during elicitation. If an elicitation participant uses words like *only*, *must*, *may*, or *may not*, they might have a business rule in mind. Asking "why" a few times can get to the source of the rule. The process of eliciting business rules sometimes reveals previously unidentified stakeholders, as well.

Data models, such as entity relationship diagrams, are good places to look for business rules. The numerical relationships—cardinalities—between data objects often are defined by business rules. Using data models in elicitation sessions will prompt conversations to understand the relevant rules.

Some business rules influence specific use cases or user stories. Attempting to violate a rule during execution constitutes an exception that the system must prevent or handle. To avoid having an unhandled exception that causes problems, the BA should write requirements to describe the system's behavior if the rule were to be violated. In some cases, stakeholders can invent rules that pertain to the solution they're building. Certain rules that come up during these explorations might affect only manual business processes; the software solution must enforce others.

Business rules might dictate that certain people are not allowed to take certain actions or access particular system functions. During requirements discussions, listen for requirements to which permissions, privilege levels, responsibilities, or prerequisites could apply. One company established this rule:

SHOW-1. Product suppliers may not attend a trade show unless they are exhibiting.

This also could be stated as:

SHOW-1. Product suppliers may attend a trade show only if they are exhibiting.

In either phrasing, the rule constrains who can attend the trade show, imposing specific conditions that suppliers must satisfy before they can get in the door. It's a good general practice to avoid negatives ("may not"), and particularly double and triple negatives, in both rules and requirements whenever possible. Try to recast negative statements as positives, which often brings in the constraining word "only."

Keep in mind that asking stakeholders "What are your business rules?" during an elicitation discussion won't be too helpful. Stakeholders aren't thinking, "Is this piece of information a business rule, a user story, or what?" They don't care; it's just important information they need to convey. It's up to the BA to sort through the diverse input received during elicitation, specify each item in an appropriate style, and store each in the right container.

Documenting Business Rules

Writing good business rules is much like writing good requirements. They should be clear, complete, correct, consistent, necessary, unambiguous, and verifiable. Rules can also have attributes associated with them, such as their effective date, the source of the rule, and its current owner or custodian.

Rules also are subject to the same problems that can afflict requirements. One rule could conflict or overlap with another. A rule might be obsolete or based on assumptions that are no longer valid. Rules could be imprecise or fail to cover certain conditions, such as boundary values in a numerical range. For instance, a retail business might have rules stating the return policies for items purchased less than 30 days ago and more than 30 days ago, but not say what happens at exactly 30 days.

Textual rules aren't always the best way to communicate information. Suppose your online store offers various combinations of discounts and free shipping depending on the total price of an order and whether the customer is a club member.

You could write out all those rules in natural language, but displaying them in the form of a decision table like the one in Figure 5.3 is easier to understand (Gottesdiener 2005, Wiegers 2020a). For example, rule DISC-5 states that if the order total is in the $50–$100 range, inclusive, and the customer is a club member, then they get a 10 percent discount and free shipping. Representing business logic with decision tables helps avoid boundary value problems and missing logical combinations. The compact table format is easier to create, read, and modify than a repetitive set of textual rules. A decision table—or its visual counterpart, a decision tree—also facilitates test design to ensure that no condition combinations are missed.

Rule ID	DISC-1	DISC-2	DISC-3	DISC-4	DISC-5	DISC-6
Conditions						
Order total	<$50	$50–$100	>$100	<$50	$50–$100	>$100
Club member	N	N	N	Y	Y	Y
Action						
No discount	x			x		
10% discount		x	x		x	
20% discount						x
Free shipping			x	x	x	x

Figure 5.3 *A decision table shows how various combinations of conditions lead to different actions or outcomes.*

Applying Business Rules

Business rules serve as the origin of functionality and data that are needed to make sure a software system complies with each rule. It's a good practice to trace requirements that were derived from a specific rule back to that rule using a technique like the requirements mapping matrix that was described in Table 4.1 (Beatty and Chen 2012). This connection is helpful if someone questions why the requirement is the way it is, as well as when rules change. A modified business rule often triggers updates in software requirements, tests, databases, and anything else that's logically connected to the rule.

As an illustration, Karl's bank charges a monthly service fee unless he maintains a specific combined minimum balance in certain types of accounts, not including his business checking account. The minimum-balance policies change from time to time, so Karl must revise his money management strategy to avoid fees. The bank must update its software systems whenever those policies change. A network of traces between individual rules and the software that enforces them helps the maintainers respond accurately and efficiently to a rule change.

If developers know which rules or what types of computations will change frequently, they can make design choices that lead to easier modifications. Consider airline flight fares, for example. Each airline has countless policies and algorithms regarding how to calculate ticket fares and related fees, and they change all the time. Maybe the passenger must pay fifty dollars to check their first piece of luggage, unless the passenger has a business-class or first-class ticket, has premium frequent-flier status, purchased a promotional upgrade package, or who knows what else. Designing a program to handle such volatility by simply updating database entries makes it a lot easier to evolve than if those rules are embedded in the code.

You can manage a small set of business rules and their connections to a software system manually, but more complex situations require automated support. If you use a requirements management tool, you can use a rationale or origin attribute to trace derived requirements to their source business rule wherever it's stored. Business rules engines let you store and manage large rule sets (Malak 2022). You can tie the rules to business workflows, specific data objects, or decision logic. The engines assist the software with making decisions by pulling together all the rules that apply to a specific scenario, such as deciding whether to approve a bank customer's loan application. Employing a business rules engine helps to keep business logic from being entwined with application code.

Business rules start as policies for how the business operates, not as software requirements. Many of them lead to functional and data requirements, though. Rules are therefore a critical piece of the requirements puzzle on every project.

Related Practices

Practice #6. Understand what users need to do with the solution.

Practice #7. Identify events and responses.

Practice #8. Assess data concepts and relationships.

Practice #10. Analyze requirements and requirement sets.

Practice #17. Create a glossary.

Next Steps

1. Identify all the pertinent business rules for your current application so that you know how they affect the requirements and design approaches. Record which functional and data requirements trace back to specific rules as their rationale or origin.

2. If other systems supply data to yours, or vice versa, look for any business rules from that application that may affect your solution.

3. If any of your business rules use combinations of multiple conditions to determine an outcome, create a decision table to ensure that you have captured all possible combinations and their actions or outcomes.

4. Establish a storage mechanism and format for recording your organization's business rules. Think of a scheme for uniquely identifying business rules so that team members can refer to them in various documents and locate the correct rules to guide their construction and testing activities.

Practice #17   Create a glossary.

Business analysis is primarily a communication challenge, not a technical or computing challenge. It's subject to all the shortcomings of both verbal and written communication. A common vocabulary helps the participants avoid misunderstandings. Therefore, each project should accumulate a glossary of significant terms, abbreviations, acronyms, and synonyms to make sure that everyone understands them in the same way, beginning at the start of the initiative.

If your organization creates a family of related products or works with the same customers repeatedly, a project's glossary could evolve into an enterprise-level glossary that you can reuse on multiple projects. Each project could begin with that global glossary, pare it down ("shrink to fit"), and add any additional items that are specific to the present endeavor. Ensure that new or changed definitions in the project glossary are updated in the enterprise glossary.

Glossary entries could include terms and jargon that pertain to the business or application domain, stakeholder roles, and project team roles. Don't try to include every term from every project in the enterprise glossary, just those that span projects. Reconcile any synonyms or conflicting definitions that arise from different sources. Establish mechanisms for broadly sharing this collected glossary and keeping it current.

Synchronizing Communication

In face-to-face conversations, we rely on context, shared experience, and body language to ensure that people reach a mutual understanding. If you're talking to someone who furrows their brow when you mention a certain word, you can tell they're puzzled and promptly clear up the confusion. That doesn't work with written communication or when speakers can't see one another; we must use more precise language.

While reviewing a requirements specification for a machine to perform chemical analyses, Karl noticed that it referred to *chemical samples* in some places and to *runs* in others. When he inquired about the difference, the author acknowledged, "They're the same thing." A requirements specification is not a good place to creatively vary your language to try to hold the reader's interest. Karl recommended that they pick a single term, define it in the glossary, and use it consistently. Otherwise, every reader will confront that same question: Are these two things the same or different? The glossary should include synonyms that different stakeholders might use in their workplace, but the requirements documentation should use terminology consistently.

Two terms in another specification looked like they might mean the same thing. When Karl asked, though, he learned that they had subtle, yet significant, distinctions. People needed to use the right term to convey information accurately. Precise glossary definitions would have helped there, as well.

Depending on the business domain, there could be a lot of synonyms and near-synonyms. If your business is a physical or online store, is there a difference between a *customer, visitor, buyer, purchaser*, and *member*? Do all the departments in your organization think of a *customer* in the same way? Does your restaurant differentiate between *guests, customers, patrons*, and *diners*? If you're an employer, how do you refer to the people who work for your company: *employee, associate, team member, staff member, cast member*? Are an *order, request, cart*, and *ticket* the same thing? It's important to carefully distinguish such terms where they appear in your business and software documents. A glossary serves as the definitive resource for all that information, aids database design, and can even help developers make their code more understandable.

Glossaries can ensure that the same term or phrase means the same thing to everyone. On one of Candase's projects, the BA team had tagged certain requirements as being "no regrets" work. This term meant that, even though the team didn't know all the requirements yet, they knew they'd need that set and would not regret building them now. However, release after release, the vendor who was developing the software kept deferring these no-regrets items. Eventually, Candase's team discovered that the vendor interpreted "no regrets" to mean there would be no regrets if they *didn't* deliver those requirements and so left them at the bottom of their priority list. An entry in the glossary—or perhaps even having a conversation rather than making assumptions—could have avoided all that confusion.

Data models are good places to look for potential glossary entries. The boxes in a data model represent important nouns, objects of interest to the project. The specific attributes of each such object appear in the data dictionary, but the corresponding glossary entries will tell you what they mean. On one project to build a learning management system, people were using the terms *training*, *curriculum*, *course*, and *class*. Discussing these closely related items with the help of a data model clarified the differences between them and revealed that some were synonyms but others were not. Storing such knowledge in a glossary prevents future confusion.

Other important terms have domain-specific meanings that differ from how the words are used in another context or in daily conversation. Some terms could even have multiple meanings within the application's context: a *printer* is both an electronic device and a person who prints something. A single abbreviation or acronym can stand for many things, yet all the project participants need to understand which one pertains to your project context. Figure 5.4 illustrates some entries from a project glossary.

Term	Definition
Active Directory (AD) Group	A group of users that can be tied to application permissions
CMS	Customer Management System: contains all customer data
COGS	Cost of Goods Sold: the direct costs attributable to the production of the goods sold in a company
Depreciation	A reduction in the value of an asset with the passage of time, due in particular to wear and tear
MBI	Minimum Business Increment: a piece of functionality that has standalone business value
NPV	Net Present Value: the value of a sum of money today, in contrast to some future value it will have when it has been invested at compound interest, net of the initial investment amount
Service-Level Agreement (SLA)	A contract between a service provider and its internal or external customers that documents what services the provider will furnish and defines the service standards the provider is obligated to meet

Figure 5.4 *A portion of a project glossary that defines important terms, abbreviations, and acronyms.*

The effort you put into building, maintaining, and referring to a glossary helps all those who write, discuss, or do work based on the requirements stay in sync. As new people join your team, the glossary can save the time otherwise spent explaining the same things over and over. A glossary is an investment in clear and effective communication, which you'll recall is an overarching goal of all requirements work.

Related Practices

Practice #14. Write requirements in consistent ways.

Practice #15. Organize requirements in a structured fashion.

Next Steps

1. Define the specialized terms that pertain to your application domain. Ask knowledgeable project participants, business collaborators, and others to review the definitions for accuracy. Invite some prospective users of the information who aren't already expert in the vocabulary to review the terms and point out any they don't fully understand.

2. Incorporate the terms from step #1 into a project glossary and make it available to all those who need to know the definitions.

3. Use your project glossary as the starting point for an enterprise-level glossary that could apply to multiple projects. Solicit contributions from other projects.

4. Create a supplemental glossary with definitions of various requirements engineering and business analysis terms. Those in Table 1.1 provide a good starting point, but your local terminology might be different. Share these definitions with user representatives, new team members, and other participants who don't already know the terminology.

Chapter 6

Requirements Validation

By this point in the requirements development process, you understand the project's business objectives. You've elicited requirements for some portion of the solution from various stakeholders, analyzed them, and recorded those requirements in appropriate forms. The team is now ready to begin development on that portion, right? Maybe.

Yes, you have some requirements—but how do you know they're the *right* requirements? Are you confident they'll meet the users' goals and address the business situation that led to launching the initiative in the first place? You could have a set of beautifully written and modeled requirements that appear to be crystal clear, complete, and unambiguous—and yet they could still be wrong. Requirements validation activities assess whether a solution that's based on an approved set of requirements would indeed satisfy stakeholder needs and achieve the intended business objectives.

A software team can confirm that the code passes its unit, integration, and system tests, that the code correctly implements the design, and that the design addresses all the requirements. Those are all software *verification* activities. However, the team can't confirm on their own that they have the correct solution requirements. That is, they cannot *validate* the requirements. Colloquially put, verification checks to see whether you did something right; validation checks to see whether you did the right thing.

One validation technique, of course, is to build the product and then collect customer feedback to see how you did. That's expensive and time-consuming. Alternatively, you can build just a portion of a solution, such as the first iteration or two of an agile team's work, and use it to learn more from your users and make course corrections. Cheaper yet is to develop prototypes to explore requirements uncertainties. But there are ways to validate requirements without writing code or waiting until the end of a development cycle.

Validation is a continuous process that begins when you have some requirements in hand. Requirements validation is interwoven with the ongoing elicitation, analysis, and specification activities. The goal is to correct problems with requirements early to reduce the risk of performing unnecessary development rework. The fuzzier the business problem and the more uncertain the solution requirements, the more important it is to validate those requirements before the team invests too much effort in implementing them. This chapter describes two powerful ways to validate requirements:

Practice #18. Review and test the requirements.

| **Practice #18** | Review and test the requirements. |

Requirements validation is important because it's so much cheaper—and less painful—to find and fix software errors early rather than later during development or following deployment (Wiegers 2022). Requirements validation is a collaborative effort: Customer representatives and other knowledgeable stakeholders are the ultimate arbiters of requirements correctness. Two valuable validation practices are peer reviews of requirements and testing requirements.

Note that "signing off" on a set of requirements is not the same thing as validating them. Signing off is an approval action, based on the expectation that the requirements are correct and the desire to get on with building the solution. In contrast, validation gives the stakeholders confidence that the team is on track for a successful delivery.

Requirements Reviews

Peer review of documented requirements is a powerful quality practice. In a peer review, colleagues of the person who created a requirements artifact examine it carefully for potential defects and other issues. A business analyst might invite another analyst to review their requirements because the other BA knows what kinds of problems to look for. However, that other BA can't tell if the requirements properly address the business need. To validate the requirements, you also need reviewers who supplied the information that led to those requirements, such as

- representatives of various user classes,
- marketing staff (for a commercial product),

- the author of any higher-level or predecessor deliverable, such as a system requirements specification, and

- subject matter experts who are familiar with pertinent business rules and other constraints.

People who must base their work on the requirements also make good reviewers even if they can't validate the requirements' correctness for meeting stakeholder needs. Architects, software and user experience designers, data analysts, developers, and testers will all find distinct kinds of issues. Testers are particularly skilled at detecting unverifiable requirements, ambiguities, and missing information. These quality reviews are important. You can't validate requirements that are unclear, inconsistent, or ambiguous because you don't know exactly what they mean.

Teams can review requirements specified in any form, in several ways (Wiegers 2002).

- In a *peer deskcheck*, a BA asks a colleague to read some requirements they wrote or examine a diagram they drew and offer feedback. These informal reviews are quick and inexpensive ways to bring another pair of eyes to the problem.

- During a *passaround*, the BA distributes the material they'd like reviewed to several participants, who examine it independently and pass their observations to the BA. Using an online review tool lets the participants see and respond to one another's comments.

- In a *team review*, the BA provides a package of requirements and background materials to several reviewers and gives them time to go through the contents on their own. During that individual preparation, reviewers note possible errors and other issues they want to raise during a review meeting. During the meeting, the reviewers pool their observations and comments, often discovering new defects during the discussion.

- An *inspection* is the most rigorous form of peer review (Gilb and Graham 1993, Wiegers 2002). Inspection participants perform specific roles and follow a defined process. The inspectors use checklists of common requirement problems to help them discover issues. You may download a requirements review checklist from the website that accompanies this book. Inspection is the most expensive and time-consuming type of peer review, but it's also a highly effective way to find many types of defects, particularly ambiguities.

Any requirements review is tedious. However, they can save considerable time later by preventing unnecessary rework and avoiding customer disappointment.

To make your reviews more effective, learn about the challenges of requirements reviews (Wiegers 2020b) and factors that can help make them successful (Wiegers 2019). Combine quick, incremental informal reviews during requirements development with inspections that closely examine the higher-risk requirements.

Testing the Requirements

When Karl was the lead BA on an information systems project, he documented several use cases from their largest user class. Next, he derived a set of functional requirements that would allow users to execute one of the use cases. Then he returned to the use case and wrote some tests that would verify whether the use case was functioning as intended. Comparing the outputs from these two thought processes revealed several errors: missing, wrong, or unneeded requirements; missing, wrong, or unneeded tests; missing information; and requirements that could be interpreted in more than one way.

For instance, Karl thought of a test that described how he expected the software would behave in a specific scenario. But when he looked for the requirements that would make this result happen, no combination or sequence of functionality could yield the result he expected. Either the test was invalid, or some functional requirements were missing.

This experience revealed two valuable lessons. First, you can begin testing your "software" as soon as you define your first requirement. And second, if you create only a single representation—one view—of the requirements, you must trust it to be correct. If you create more than one view, perhaps in separate brains, you can compare them and find disconnects. Karl became an enthusiastic fan of testing his requirements before he wrote any code, and he discovered errors every time he did.

A related idea comes from Suzanne Robertson and James Robertson (2013). They speak of writing *fit criteria* to ensure that a requirement is sufficiently well understood. The fit criteria describe how to determine if a requirement is correctly addressed in the solution. Fit criteria should be measurable, such as response times, or otherwise verifiable, as with acceptance tests that describe the solution's behavior under defined conditions.

Engage testers in the requirements process early. Suppose a tester writes a test from a use case that conflicts with a functional requirement that a BA derived from the same use case. The use case might contain ambiguous language that led to two different interpretations. Testers are fiendishly skillful at thinking of ways to break software. They can conceive tests that would fail because a requirement doesn't describe how to handle some exception or edge case they identified.

The tests you write against requirements are black-box tests. You don't need to know anything about the internal structure of a potential solution—indeed, you don't have a solution yet. Your tests are at a conceptual level, independent of implementation and user interface specifics. You can use these conceptual tests to validate any form of requirements representation, including text, models, and prototypes.

During requirements validation, work with your user representatives to understand how they would conclude whether a solution was acceptable for their purposes, and then write acceptance criteria, including tests, to document that information. Trace each test back to its corresponding requirement—a user story, use case, functional requirement, or quality attribute requirement. Tracing requirements to tests helps if a requirement changes, as the trace data points to those tests that might have to be updated.

Acceptance Criteria

Agile teams often write user acceptance criteria in the form of acceptance tests to define a user story's details, rather than documenting the functional requirements that would realize the story. This technique is an element of Test-Driven Development or TDD (Beck 2003), Acceptance Test-Driven Development or ATDD (Hendrickson 2008), Behavior-Driven Development or BDD (North 2006), and Specification by Example or SBE (Adzic 2011). Users who contribute to this activity might find tests to be a helpful way to envision whether a story will meet their needs, which is the essence of requirements validation. Acceptance criteria could also include other conditions the solution must satisfy beyond passing its tests.

A popular pattern for writing acceptance tests uses the *Given–When–Then* pattern (Fowler 2013):

Given *<specific preconditions that are true>*

When *<some action, behavior, or event takes place>*

Then *<this is what should happen as a consequence>*

Any or all of the three clauses in this pattern could be compound, with multiple preconditions, actions, and/or consequences separated by AND. However, use caution if AND appears in the When clause of a Given–When–Then acceptance test. A compound action often means that some information in the When clause really describes preconditions that should more properly appear in the Given clause. Candase has found this situation to be especially common for acceptance tests that don't involve users but involve data preconditions and system event actions.

As an example of using Given–When–Then, let's return to a user story for the imaginary publishing platform Speak-Out.biz from Practice #6, "Understand what users need to do with the solution":

> As an author, I want to view the page-view statistics for my published articles so that I can see which topics my readers enjoy the most.

Table 6.1 shows several acceptance tests for this story, written in the Given–When–Then format and laid out in a tabular format. These tests flesh out the expected behaviors associated with that user story just as functional requirements do. Requirements and tests are two complementary ways to describe the same solution knowledge: what the team is supposed to build and how it is supposed to behave.

Table 6.1 *Several acceptance tests for a user story in the Given–When–Then format*

ID	Given	When	Then
AT-1	I am logged in to the platform AND I have articles published	I request to view statistics	A graph of my total article view statistics from the past 30 days is displayed AND a list of statistics (views, reads, and likes) for individual articles is displayed in reverse chronological order by publication date
AT-2	I am logged in to the platform AND I do not have articles published	I request to view statistics	A message appears: You haven't published any articles yet
AT-3	Statistics are displayed	I request to change the sort order for any statistics column	The statistics display toggles between ascending and descending order based on the values in the selected column

Another way to document tests is in the form of a decision table (Wiegers 2020a). As we saw in Practice #16, "Identify and document business rules," a decision table is an efficient way to depict all the combinations of conditions that can lead to various outcomes. Decision tables help ensure thorough test coverage without writing a lot of bulky and repetitive text.

Testing Analysis Models

Suppose you've drawn a model to complement some of your requirements. You can trace the logical "execution" path on the model with a highlighter pen as you walk through the tests to see if the system would behave as you expect. After you go through all the tests with your highlighter, look for problems. A path in the model that isn't highlighted could indicate either that you're missing a test or that the path doesn't reflect a legitimate system behavior. If a test has no corresponding path to trace in the model, either the test is incorrect or the model is incomplete. Either way, the disconnect tells you there's a problem.

Here's an example. Figure 4.4 showed a process flow for a website to let sales representatives enter orders for a customer who's on the phone. Figure 6.1 shows a portion of that process flow, which the BA drew based on their initial understanding of the business process. In one scenario, the customer's requested items are all out of stock. Among many others, the tester has written the following test:

Given that the cart is empty

When the customer declines to order more items

Then the process terminates.

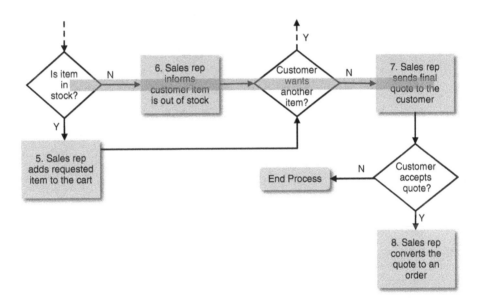

Figure 6.1 *A portion of the process flow for a sales representative adding items to the cart for a customer who's on the phone.*

If you attempt to trace the path this test describes on the process flow in Figure 6.1, as shown with the gray highlight, you can't do it. The diagram says that if the requested items are not in stock and the customer doesn't want to order more items, thereby leaving the cart empty, the sales rep still sends the final, empty quote to the customer. Clearly, that's an error in the model and in any textual requirements that align with the model.

The BA redraws that portion of the model to look like Figure 6.2, to check whether the cart contains items following the end of the customer–sales rep dialogue. Now you can trace that test's path correctly on the process flow diagram, ending the sales process instead of sending the customer a meaningless quote. Finding errors *before* the team writes the code and the customer encounters a problem is a good thing. Customers are never in a good mood when they report a problem.

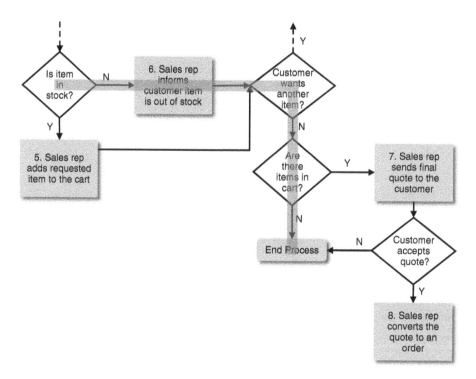

Figure 6.2 *A revised portion of the process flow that corrects an error found by "executing" a test on the model.*

Testing Requirements Efficiently

When you write tests against requirements, you face the same challenges as when you test executable software: There is potentially a vast number of test cases. You need to reduce the number of tests to a manageable size while still including all those necessary tests that could reveal errors. Two techniques that make requirements testing more efficient are the black-box testing methods *equivalence partitioning* (Sharma 2021) and *boundary value analysis* (Sharma 2022).

Equivalence partitioning divides input test conditions into categories such that the system will respond to all the test conditions in any one category in the same way: pass or fail. That way, any representative test condition in each category will yield the same information as any other. If your requirement describes how to process inputs of integers from 1 to 100, inclusive, then all integers in that range make up a single equivalence class. You can choose any one of them for a test of the whole class. Other equivalence classes would be integers outside this range and nonintegers.

Boundary value analysis examines system behavior at the partitions between equivalence classes that are based on numeric ranges. If you're testing the range of integers from 1 to 100, inclusive, boundary value analysis would include tests with values 0, 1, 2, 99, 100, and 101. Four of those values—1, 2, 99, and 100—are in the same equivalence class, but boundary value errors are so common, both in requirements and in code, that it doesn't hurt to check those areas more carefully.

Pushing Quality to the Front

It might appear that working on tests while you're still developing requirements is premature and duplicated testing effort. It is not. The conceptual tests you create to validate requirements can evolve into specific test scripts and procedures to verify the implemented solution. You don't have to re-invent all those tests, just build on them.

In addition, all requirements verification and validation activities are a way to push quality to the front of the development cycle's timeline, where the greatest leverage lies. As Figure 6.3 shows, reallocating some testing effort to the requirements activities yields higher-quality requirements, which leads to less rework later and improved stakeholder satisfaction. Reducing rework is a key to higher productivity (Wiegers 2022). Everybody wins.

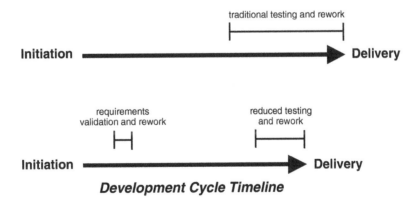

Figure 6.3 *Reallocating some testing effort to requirements validation reduces late-stage testing and rework for a net time savings.*

Related Practices

Practice #6. Understand what users need to do with the solution.

Practice #11. Create requirements models.

Practice #12. Create and evaluate prototypes.

Next Steps

1. Identify portions of your requirements that are more likely to have problems than others. Perhaps those sections didn't have adequate stakeholder input or are especially complex or risky. Select some people who could provide insight into how to assess those areas. Invite them to review the requirements so that the team has confidence that they'll meet the stakeholders' needs.

2. When you write some new requirements, ask a tester to create acceptance tests from them. Walk through those tests and map them to your written requirements and analysis models to look for discrepancies.

3. Identify the equivalence classes for testing a particular feature in your application. See if certain test conditions could be satisfied efficiently using just one test.

Chapter 7

Requirements Management

The previous chapters described eighteen practices that lay the foundation for a successful project and help you develop a set of high-quality solution requirements. Once you have those fine requirements in hand, now what happens to them? Requirements management is the subdomain of requirements engineering that deals with how requirements are used on the project and how the project responds to evolving needs.

In an ideal world, the development team would take the set of requirements developed for some portion of the product, implement them into a solution, and then move directly on to the requirements for the next portion. In the real world, requirements are dynamic. Understanding deepens and changes, markets and businesses evolve, and new requirements come along. Some planned requirements are deferred, others turn out to be incorrect or unnecessary, and stakeholders adjust priorities. The BA and development team must respond to this ongoing stream of modifications, keeping everything straight along the way. Major requirements management activities include these (Wiegers and Beatty 2013):

- Defining requirements baselines, those sets of requirements that are committed to a particular development cycle, product release, or maintenance activity

- Requirements version control, which involves tracking evolving versions of both individual requirements and requirement sets

- Tracking requirement status as each one moves through its life cycle from being proposed to ultimately being verified as correctly implemented in the product, deferred, or deleted from a baseline and archived

- Tracing requirements backward to their origin and forward to their associated design elements, code segments, tests, and other connected requirements

- Receiving new requirements and changes requested in existing ones and then folding those appropriately into planned development activities

While all these activities are valuable, many teams will perform them selectively. For instance, it's easy to trace tests back to individual functional requirements, use cases, or user stories. However, building a complete requirements traceability matrix takes effort and discipline (Wiegers and Beatty 2013). It requires tool support, established processes, and time. Most projects probably won't do full traceability, although it is required for safety-critical products that must be certified prior to release and other solutions that are subject to regulatory requirements. Certifiers and other stakeholders need to know that each bit of functionality was designed, coded, and tested as intended. Full requirements tracing for your average business information system or phone app is desirable—and we recommend it for most projects—but less essential.

This final chapter addresses two requirements management practices that do affect every project:

Practice #19. Establish and manage requirements baselines.

Practice #20. Manage changes to requirements effectively.

Practice #19   Establish and manage requirements baselines.

As the business analyst, you've developed a set of requirements and confirmed that they describe a solution that will address your business objectives. The next step is for the development team to identify a subset of those requirements that they can commit to implementing in a specific time frame or development cycle: a requirements baseline.

Requirements Baseline Defined

We are using the word *baseline* here in two senses. The first sense refers to an agreed-upon set of requirements that's approved for a specific development cycle and serves as the basis for subsequent work. The second sense refers to the software that the team builds during that cycle based on those requirements.

A baseline cements a group of requirements as a snapshot in time. It says that, to the best of everyone's knowledge at that time, those requirements are correct, are complete, and will contribute to achieving the desired business outcomes. Baselining low-quality requirements doesn't do anybody any good, so consider the factors that let you judge whether a set of requirements is ready to go before you baseline them (Wheatcraft 2015). Any changes to requirements that are requested after they are baselined must go through the team's change control process. Approving those changes establishes a new baseline (see Practice #20, "Manage changes to requirements effectively"). Defining a requirements baseline enables

- stakeholders to understand the scope that's planned for upcoming iterations,
- the development team to estimate size and the resources needed for that baseline,
- the quality assurance team to finalize their tests, and
- the development team to make delivery commitments.

Establishing a requirements baseline does not mean change won't happen; it will. However, a baseline assures everyone involved that the team can move forward with development at a low risk of major changes (Inflectra 2020).

A baseline can be as small as a two-week iteration or as large as a release or even an entire solution scope. The act of baselining can be informal or formal. The size or formality is less important than having the stakeholders explicitly agree on the scope of the baseline and that the team is ready to proceed with implementation. The baseline for a portion of a solution could include a mix of software functionality, manual operations, and business processes. All the interrelated elements must be delivered for that part of the solution to be useful.

Two Baselining Strategies

When defining a requirements baseline, the team has two major options: time bound or scope bound. A time-bound baseline begins by establishing a time box: an iteration, a group of iterations, or a scheduled release. The team then allocates the highest-priority requirements from their requirements set or product backlog of pending work to the baseline until the time box's development and testing capacities have been filled (see Practice #13, "Prioritize the requirements"). This approach requires the development and testing teams either to have already sized the requirements so that they can know when capacity is filled, or to perform sizing as part of the baselining activity. Time-bound baselines are most common on agile projects in which each iteration has a requirements baseline, although release-based iterative projects can use them as well.

Scope-bound baselines, in contrast, consist of a logically grouped set of features, requirements, or user stories that can be built, tested, and deployed together and are approved as a unit. With the scope-bound approach, the requirements baseline is established without necessarily knowing its size or delivery schedule. Development and testing teams will then estimate the size of the requirements in the baseline to make timeline estimates and delivery commitments.

Sometimes the estimates are higher than expected or higher than is acceptable. Then the team must reduce the scope to create a new baseline with an earlier delivery date, or more resources must be provided, or the stakeholders must agree to the currently estimated delivery date. (Well, another option is to cut quality in the rush to deliver the full scope, but we think that's a bad idea.)

Most teams use only one of the two bounding strategies to define their baselines. Work with your stakeholders and development team to decide which approach best suits your organization and product. Your project type and development life cycle will largely drive the size and nature of your baselines. Regardless of its size, a baseline's importance lies in aligning all parties in agreement on a set of requirements and delivery commitments. Establishing a requirements baseline is a form of expectation management.

Identifying Which Requirements Are Included in a Baseline

You need to uniquely identify those requirements that are proposed for a given baseline. One option is to place a subset of requirements from a software requirements specification (SRS) into a new SRS to define the baseline for a specific development cycle (Wiegers 2006). If you're using a requirements management tool, you can add metadata (attributes) to the selected requirements to indicate which baseline or release they belong to. On an agile project, you might allocate stories to a given iteration in a tool. That set of stories then becomes the baseline proposal that the team considers during iteration planning. In any case, ensure that everyone can unambiguously find the requirements that form the baseline proposal by document location, database query, or iteration definition.

Some of the diagrams described in Practice #11, "Create requirements models," can depict requirements baselines at a higher level of abstraction. Executives find it useful to see what functionality is intended for which release in a one-page view. For example, you can annotate or color-code the elements of a context diagram (see Figure 2.5) to illustrate which integrations to external systems will be built when. Similarly, you can highlight elements of a data flow diagram or entity relationship diagram to show the processes and data objects that make up each baseline for upcoming development cycles.

You can also identify a scope baseline using a feature tree or in a feature roadmap (Wiegers 2006). Figure 7.1 is a revised version of the feature tree from Figure 4.2 for the restaurant online ordering site. The circled numbers next to certain level 2 and level 3 subfeatures indicate their planned release number; subfeatures that are not numbered inherit their parent feature's release number. The baseline for the first release, then, consists of all the features and subfeatures tagged with the number 1. As illustrated in Figure 7.1, even though the team will build the site and integrate it with the existing restaurant order placement system and menu repository in the first release, certain subfeatures under Order Placement and Online Menu will be deferred to later releases. Other ways to depict the scope of the various releases with the feature tree include using layers or colors in a tool like Microsoft Visio or Lucidchart.

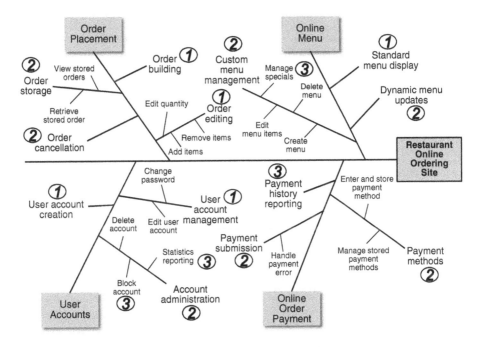

Figure 7.1 *You can overlay planned iterations, releases, or requirements baseline versions on the elements in a feature tree.*

Getting Agreement on the Baseline

To make any baseline official, the BA must obtain agreement on it from all relevant stakeholders. These could include the development and quality assurance teams, user class representatives, marketing, important customers, and/or management representatives. Approving a baseline can be simple and informal, such as an agile team agreeing to a list of user stories for a single iteration. A larger baseline will likely go through a formal approval process that requires a review meeting and a documented sign-off from each representative (Wheatcraft 2015).

Work with your team to agree on the process you'll follow to document and approve a requirements baseline. All participants need to know what is expected of them when approving a baseline and the date by which their approval is needed to keep the project moving. Determine how you'll record and store the approvals: an approvals table in a document, attributes in a requirements management tool, or perhaps the status of a story for the current iteration in the backlog tool. On an agile project, any stories proposed for an iteration baseline that are not approved for development are returned to the product backlog for consideration in future iterations.

Occasionally you may encounter stakeholders who won't approve a baseline in a timely manner. They might fear that agreeing to the baseline means that they can't alter those requirements thereafter. Development teams that are unsure if they can deliver all the requested requirements on schedule could be reluctant to make a commitment. An obvious option is to present approvers with an ultimatum stating that their approval will be assumed after a certain date even without their explicit agreement. A better approach is to work with each group to pinpoint the underlying reasons for not approving the baseline. If the worry is not being able to ask for changes after approval, point them to your documented change process to assure them that change is possible (and hopefully not onerous). Simply asking "What would it take for you to approve the baseline?" is a way to start the discussion.

Candase has worked with several agile teams in which the developers hesitated to commit to the full story list for an iteration because of known complexities or remaining unknowns. In those instances, the team tagged some user stories as stretch goals, with the iteration's baseline containing only the committed stories. The stretch goals became preapproved extensions to the baseline in case the development team could fit them in. If the development team could not deliver the stretch goals, they were deferred back to the product backlog and discussed in future iteration planning sessions based on their priority. This process allowed the team to agree to the iteration's baseline while streamlining future baselining through the preapproval.

If the stakeholders still won't approve the baseline—and you're sure they're the right approvers—point out the risk that their lack of approval adds to development moving forward. If the risk is minimal, document their lack of approval and its implications (potentially missed or incorrect requirements), and cautiously proceed with the defined baseline. If the risk is high that the team will build an incorrect solution without some stakeholder's approval, continue working with them until you either obtain their approval or revise the baseline to one they find acceptable.

Managing Multiple Baselines and Changes to Them

Once a baseline has been approved, the BA must manage changes to it. Whenever a new or modified requirement is approved through your change control process, you should establish a new baseline snapshot. Agree with your team where the baseline definitions will be stored (a tool or a document) and how you will identify the current baseline for an iteration or release. Continue updating the baseline as necessary through your change control process until the team deploys it to users.

You might have multiple baselines in progress at any given time. Candase typically deals with at least two baselines in parallel: one that has been developed and is being tested by users or external quality assurance, and one that is still in development (Figure 7.2). As changes come in, make sure you know which baseline each applies to, so all team members always know what they are—and are not—supposed to be working on.

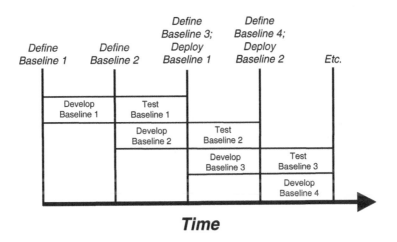

Figure 7.2 *A BA could be managing multiple baselines concurrently to support both development and testing efforts.*

Some teams build their solution in defined development iterations but do not deliver the product from each iteration to users for any of several possible reasons. Instead, they integrate the outputs from several iterations and deploy the resultant solution as a product release. In that situation, you might define an overall requirements baseline for the release, as well as defining a baseline of allocated and approved requirements for each iteration.

Figure 7.3 shows how this approach might work for a release that incorporates three iterations. The product owner or BA may modify stories or move them between iterations as long as they're still part of the overall release baseline. Keeping the release and iteration baselines updated would indicate the stories currently planned for each iteration. There's a chance that what the team delivers won't exactly match what was planned for a particular baseline; in reality, that's just how software development works. Therefore, it's a good idea to update the initial requirements baseline documentation (the plan) to reflect what the team actually built (the reality) whenever they differ (Hokanson and Szymanski 2022).

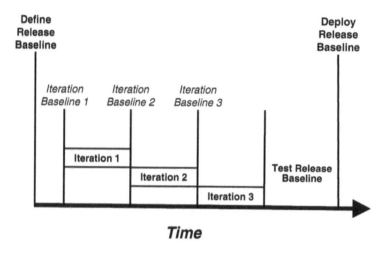

Figure 7.3 *Multiple iteration baselines can be bundled into a release baseline.*

Regardless of the size, type, number, or formality of your baselines, aligning stakeholders on the scope to be implemented is a critical precursor for beginning or continuing development. Establishing a requirements baseline formally initiates the change control process. Managing that baseline through to deployment ensures that everyone involved understands what the team will deliver to its stakeholders.

Related Practices

Practice #5. Identify empowered decision makers.

Practice #11. Create requirements models.

Practice #13. Prioritize the requirements.

Practice #20. Manage changes to requirements effectively.

Next Steps

1. Work with your development team and key stakeholders to understand your current requirements baseline. If it is not documented, record the contents in some fashion. If the team has begun development of a baseline that was not approved, work with the relevant stakeholders to gain approval, even retroactively.

2. If your team hasn't already done so, define a process for baselining a set of requirements.

3. As new changes come into scope, be sure to update the appropriate baselines so that they remain accurate descriptions of what the team is implementing.

Practice #20	Manage changes to requirements effectively.

As we all know, change happens. Even the smartest BA with the most information at their disposal, following all the practices in this book, cannot specify perfect requirements. Even if they could, those requirements are only perfect at a particular point in time. Therefore, managing changes is one of the most important things a BA does once they have crafted a set of requirements.

Effective requirements change management ensures that the team delivers the right solution at the right time even though they didn't know everything up front. Resistance to change, especially the attitude that there will (or can) be no further changes once some requirements are baselined, can result in unusable features, disappointing releases, and unhappy stakeholders. *Baselined* doesn't mean *frozen*.

Suppose your agile team baselined the requirements for its current iteration at its planning meeting. Four days into the iteration, someone discovers that the logic for one story is incorrect. Perhaps someone made an assumption that turned out to be false or new information arrived. What do you do, how do you decide, and who decides? You have several options.

You could ask the developer to accept a change to the story if they haven't yet started or finished it, assuming the effort doesn't cause the story's implementation to extend past the iteration. Alternatively, you could complete the iteration with this story included, even though it's wrong, and fix it in a future iteration. Or you could stop development on that story, omitting it from the iteration's codebase. If work has not yet begun, you could remove the story from the current iteration, correct the logic error, and implement it in a future iteration. Your choice of action depends on the states of the story and the iteration, how critical the story is, dependencies other stories have on this one, the impact of delivering a flawed story, and the policies in your change control process.

Your goal is to manage requirements changes as they arise with as little negative impact as possible on the team's development progress. Achieving this goal requires multiple activities:

- Defining a change control process
- Following the process for all requested changes
- Identifying the decision makers
- Assessing the impact of each proposed requirement change
- Updating requirements baselines as new or changed requirements are approved
- Informing all affected stakeholders about requirement change decisions

Anticipating Requirement Changes

Change requests can originate from anyone, including customers, marketing, sales, developers, testers, product owners, regulators, and even business analysts. Users may think of something new the product could do or suggest ways to improve the user experience. Testing by quality assurance staff or users could reveal missing functionality and refine performance targets or other quality attribute goals. High-level decision makers might modify the business objectives in response to evolving market factors, which could impact the entire solution. Developers sometimes get ideas for new features they think (hope) will delight their customers. Even you, as the BA, could conceive a better approach toward solving a problem that leads to new or revised requirements.

Because change is inevitable, the BA must anticipate and be prepared to manage the flow of requirement changes, starting when the solution's boundaries are defined early in the project. During elicitation, note which functional areas are likely to evolve over time. These areas could be dominated by business rules or reflect likely product growth directions. Areas where you expect frequent modifications are candidates for configuration-based or data-based solutions rather than hardcoded solutions. You might need to include functionality to let administrators adjust the application's configurable parameters as needed.

Candase once received a requirement to show an invoice in a country's local currency even if the purchase originated in a different currency. The initial requirement was for a single country and simply converted US dollars to the local currency. However, Candase knew that the product's expansion plan included deploying to more than twenty additional countries, each with its own currency. Consequently, she generalized the requirement such that the currency to use when generating the invoice was defined via a configuration. Adding new countries then required only data and configuration changes, which are faster and simpler to make than requirement or code updates.

Plans for iterations, releases, or entire projects should always incorporate *contingency buffers* to let the team accommodate a certain amount of change and growth without disrupting schedules and commitments (Wiegers 2022). *Feeding buffers* are placed at the end of a series of dependent tasks or an iteration to provide some slack time. A *project buffer* goes at the end of the schedule for a release or an entire project. An agile project can reserve some capacity in each iteration, as well as adding a contingency buffer iteration to the end of the iteration sequence (Cohn 2006, Thomas 2008). Without buffers, the first change that comes along (or the first estimate that turns out to be low, or the first person who departs the team, or the first risk that materializes into a problem, or...) could hamper delivery commitments. Change always has a cost. Even taking the time to discuss a proposed change and then deciding not to implement it carries a price tag.

Defining the Change Control Process

Every project handles changes, whether their method is ad hoc and arbitrary or systematic and documented. Candase has experienced the full range of projects with dysfunctional change management processes. Some had none at all. This led to chaos when stakeholders revised features without notifying the product owner (PO) or development team to update the stories and then wondered why their requests weren't implemented. Other projects had such a burdensome change process that people routinely went around it. As with so many things in life, somewhere in between is a better place to be. Karl once developed a change control process for a fast-moving and overburdened development group. The team members appreciated the value that the process provided by bringing order to their ceaseless stream of requests. An effective change control process serves as a structure to manage change effectively, not as a barrier (Bals 2022).

Change control begins when a set of requirements is baselined and ends when the team delivers the solution. Each team should establish and document its change control process early on, even if it's simple. Your process should answer these questions:

- How does someone submit a change request?
- What information is required when the request is submitted? What additional information is gathered later for impact assessment?

- Are changes requested against a specific baseline, or will the appropriate baseline be determined as part of the assessment?
- Who assesses the size and impact of a change request?
- What criteria are used to approve or reject a requested change?
- Who can approve the change and allocate it to a baseline?
- How is information about the change stored once it's either approved or rejected?
- How is the decision communicated to those affected?

The change control process should be as lightweight and quick as possible, providing the right people with the necessary information to let them make good business and technical decisions (Wiegers and Beatty 2013). A small change or changes on a project with a small, colocated team can be handled simply. Perhaps the product owner and a developer just agree to modify a story in the current development iteration. In that case, the PO "submits" the change through a conversation, the PO and developer are the approvers, and the change is incorporated as a revised story or new acceptance criteria.

Changes on complex, multiteam, or distributed projects can have a broad impact and therefore demand a more formal, multistep process. Start with a simple but effective process; add complexity and layers of approval only when you find the project needs it. The decision makers constitute a *change* (or *configuration*) *control board* or CCB, which could range from just one person to a group including representatives from customers, development, testing, marketing, management, and possibly even finance.

Figure 7.4 shows a semiformal change control process that Candase has used. Most commonly, a business partner sent a change request through the team's messaging channel to initiate the process. The development team, PO, and relevant business partner served as the CCB. They considered each request based on its size, whether the team could implement it without trade-offs to defer other stories, and whether any identified trade-offs were acceptable. This evaluation and decision process typically took from one to five days to complete, depending on the change's complexity.

Change requests go through a life cycle of possible statuses (Wiegers and Beatty 2013). Each request begins with the status of submitted, after which it might be evaluated for impact. The decision makers either approve or reject it. An approved change eventually is incorporated into the solution, at which point it is verified and finally closed. The submitter could cancel a request at any point in the process. Tracking requirement change statuses makes sure that none get lost in the shuffle and that people don't work on unapproved changes because of miscommunications. Status data also lets you assess how efficiently your process resolves proposed changes.

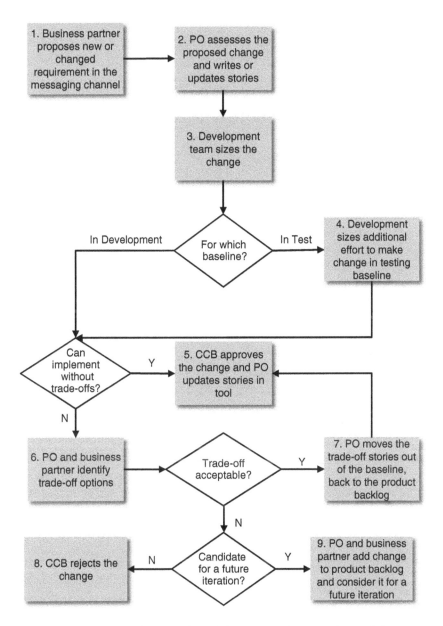

Figure 7.4 *A process flow for a semiformal change control process shows all the steps involved.*

The change control process and its sometimes-dreaded counterpart, the change control board, are not meant to make change difficult. They exist so that the decision makers have the necessary information about cost, impact, and trade-offs to make good, timely decisions. All teams must deal with changes in requirements. Those that lack a process that's defined and followed can expect more chaos, some ill-considered decisions, and unpleasant surprises.

Assessing Changes for Impacts

As with other requirements, the BA must elicit the details and analyze, specify, and validate change requests. The decision makers need certain information to determine whether to approve or reject a request. That information includes cost and effort estimates (including the time needed for requirements work on the change), priority or urgency, and a full understanding of the impact on other solution components and tasks (Wiegers and Beatty 2013, Inflectra 2020). Some changes are localized, but others can have ripple effects that extend into the ecosystem well beyond the immediate product. The BA plays a critical role in analyzing whether the change is really required, which requirements baselines or development iterations it affects, and the scope of its impact.

Candase's project team once received what appeared to be a simple request: Change the URL used to invoke a service from a vendor product to a new URL that would exploit a mechanism to prevent timeout failures. However, as she did the analysis, it became clear that this was not just a simple URL update—it required invasive revisions to three separate systems. Her analysis and the subsequent cost estimate led the decision makers to conclude that this change was too risky for the current release. They deferred it to the next release, defining a workaround in case of timeout failures in the meantime. Without that careful analysis, the team might have approved an expensive change that would have caused many headaches and delays in testing and deployment. Changes that are accepted without sufficient impact analysis might also pose a risk of failing to comply with pertinent regulations or other business rules.

Use your business objectives to assess whether the request contributes toward the project's goals; changes that don't might not be required. Analysis models such as requirements mapping and traceability matrices, process flows, ecosystem maps, and feature trees can help you quickly identify likely impacted areas from a change request (Beatty and Chen 2012). Analyze how the change would affect previously built or planned functionality. Decompose the requirements for each change to a sufficient level of detail to estimate the implementation effort in all affected areas and understand risks and dependencies.

Keep new or changed requirements separate—logically or physically—from defined baselines until they're approved. Some teams use tags in their requirements management tool to distinguish requirements that are in the baseline from change requests that are not yet approved. Other teams use a separate change request tool to collect and maintain information about the status of requested changes and to facilitate communication.

After a Decision Is Made

Approving or rejecting a request isn't the final change management action. The team must document the decision, communicate it to affected stakeholders, and update the appropriate requirements baseline if the request was approved. Documenting why a requested change was rejected can facilitate a quick response if it pops up again in the future. Updating the baseline involves revising the pertinent requirements themselves, versioning them as appropriate, updating related models, and defining a new baseline.

Managing changes in requirements can be challenging. However, the effort you expend in keeping your requirements current as change happens keeps the team members aligned toward delivering the solution the organization needs.

In Search of Less Change

You need to be able to handle changes efficiently on your project, because change is a reality in the software world. However, change always has a price and can be disruptive. Many teams spend much more time than they expected patching in new or modified functionality late in development, and then fixing all the things that broke or were overlooked from those changes.

Don't use the ability to adapt to change as an excuse for skimping on understanding needs and thinking about requirements. The many techniques described in this book can reduce the number of changes requested because of fuzzy business objectives, overlooked stakeholders, poorly understood requirements, and all the other ways requirements can go wrong.

Related Practices

Practice # 5. Identify empowered decision makers.

Practice #10. Analyze requirements and requirement sets.

Practice #13. Prioritize the requirements.

Practice #19. Establish and manage requirements baselines.

Next Steps

1. Gain an understanding of your team's current change control process. Document it if the process has not yet been written down. Draw a process flow model for your process analogous to that in Figure 7.4.

2. Make sure your change control process includes time for the BA to assess the impact of each change request. That crucial evaluation provides the information the decision makers need to approve or reject the request.

3. Assess how well your current change control process serves the team. Should it be made more structured and explicit? Or can it be simplified and streamlined? Do the right people participate? Does everyone know how to use it? Do they follow the process, or do changes slip in through the back door?

4. Examine your current requirements baseline for any unapproved changes that were incorporated without going through your change control process. Finding those changes can be a challenge if the contents of the baseline were never clearly identified. If you find any unapproved changes that have not yet been implemented, run them through your change control process. You might discover that you don't need them in the current development cycle, or maybe ever.

Appendix

Summary of Practices

Laying the Foundation

Practice #1.   Understand the problem before converging on a solution.

Practice #2.   Define business objectives.

Practice #3.   Define the solution's boundaries.

Practice #4.   Identify and characterize stakeholders.

Practice #5.   Identify empowered decision makers.

Requirements Elicitation

Practice #6.   Understand what users need to do with the solution.

Practice #7.   Identify events and responses.

Practice #8.   Assess data concepts and relationships.

Practice #9.   Elicit and evaluate quality attributes.

Requirements Analysis

Practice #10. Analyze requirements and requirement sets.

Practice #11. Create requirements models.

Practice #12. Create and evaluate prototypes.

Practice #13. Prioritize the requirements.

Requirements Specification

Practice #14. Write requirements in consistent ways.

Practice #15. Organize requirements in a structured fashion.

Practice #16. Identify and document business rules.

Practice #17. Create a glossary.

Requirements Validation

Practice #18. Review and test the requirements.

Requirements Management

Practice #19. Establish and manage requirements baselines.

Practice #20. Manage changes to requirements effectively.

References

Abba, Ihechikara Vincent. 2022. "Crow's Foot Notation—Relationship Symbols and How to Read Diagrams." https://www.freecodecamp.org/news/crows-foot-notation-relationship-symbols-and-how-to-read-diagrams.

Adams, Chris. n.d. "Agile: User Stories versus Epics, what's the difference?" https://www.modernanalyst.com/Careers/InterviewQuestions/tabid/128/ID/5086/Agile-User-Stories-versus-Epics-whats-the-difference.aspx.

Adzic, Gojko. 2011. *Specification by Example: How Successful Teams Deliver the Right Software*. Shelter Island, NY: Manning Publications Co.

Agile Alliance. 2022a. "Product Owner." https://www.agilealliance.org/glossary/product-owner.

_____. 2022b. "Minimum Viable Product (MVP)." https://www.agilealliance.org/glossary/mvp.

Alexander, Ian F., and Neil Maiden. 2004. *Scenarios, Stories, Use Cases: Through the Systems Development Life-Cycle*. Chichester, England: John Wiley & Sons, Ltd.

Alexander, Ian F., and Richard Stevens. 2002. *Writing Better Requirements*. Boston: Addison-Wesley.

Ambler, Scott W. 2005. *The Elements of UML™ 2.0 Style*. New York: Cambridge University Press.

ArgonDigital. 2022. "The Business Objectives Model Defined." https://argondigital.com/resource/tools-templates/business-objective-models.

Bals, Bernhard. 2022. "A Guide to Effective Requirements Change Management." https://www.eqmc-consulting.de/requirements-change-management.

Beatty, Joy, and Anthony Chen. 2012. *Visual Models for Software Requirements*. Redmond, WA: Microsoft Press.

Beck, Kent. 2003. *Test-Driven Development: By Example*. Boston: Addison-Wesley.

Bergman, Gustav. 2010. "A Use Case Is to a User Story as a Gazelle to a Gazebo." *Lean Magazine*. Issue #4. http://leanmagazine.net/req/a-use-case-is-to-a-user-story-as-a-gazelle-to-a-gazebo.

Bernstein, David. 2016. "The Single Wringable Neck." https://tobeagile.com/the-single-wringable-neck.

Blais, Steven P. 2012. *Business Analysis: Best Practices for Success*. Hoboken, NJ: John Wiley & Sons, Inc.

Booch, Grady, James Rumbaugh, and Ivar Jacobson. 1999. *The Unified Modeling Language User Guide*. Reading, MA: Addison-Wesley.

Brosseau, Jim. 2010. "Software Quality Attributes: Following All the Steps." https://clarrus.com/resources/articles-case-studies.

Business Analysis Excellence. n.d. "Your First Business Requirements Meeting: 8 Steps and example questions." https://business-analysis-excellence.com/business-requirements-meeting.

Capterra. n.d. "Prototyping Software." https://www.capterra.com/prototyping-software.

Cockburn, Alistair. 2001. *Writing Effective Use Cases*. Boston: Addison-Wesley.

Cohn, Mike. 2004. *User Stories Applied: For Agile Software Development*. Boston: Addison-Wesley.

_____. 2006. *Agile Estimating and Planning*. Boston: Addison-Wesley.

_____. 2012. "Two Examples of Splitting Epics." https://www.mountaingoatsoftware.com/blog/two-examples-of-splitting-epics.

Coleman, Ben, and Dan Goodwin. 2017. *Designing UX: Prototyping*. Collingwood, VIC, Australia: SitePoint Pty. Ltd.

Compton, James. 2022. "How A Problem Statement Kept Me In Control Of My Analysis." https://www.modernanalyst.com/Resources/Articles/tabid/115/ID/6094/How-A-Problem-Statement-Kept-Me-In-Control-Of-My-Analysis.aspx.

Constantine, Larry L., and Lucy A.D. Lockwood. 1999. *Software for Use: A Practical Guide to the Models and Methods of Usage-Centered Design*. Reading, MA: Addison-Wesley.

Davis, Alan M. 2005. *Just Enough Requirements Management: Where Software Development Meets Marketing*. New York: Dorset House Publishing.

Delligatti, Lenny. 2014. *SysML Distilled: A Brief Guide to the Systems Modeling Language*. Boston: Addison-Wesley.

Dutta, Nayantara. 2022. "What It's Like to Be 'Mind Blind'." https://time.com/6155443/aphantasia-mind-blind.

Feldmann, Clarence G. 1998. *The Practical Guide to Business Process Reengineering Using IDEF0*. New York: Dorset House Publishing.

Fowler, Martin. 2013. "GivenWhenThen." https://martinfowler.com/bliki/GivenWhenThen.html.

Freund, Jakob, and Bernd Rücker. 2019. *Real-Life BPMN, 4th Ed*. Independently published.

Gause, Donald C., and Brian Lawrence. 1999. "User-Driven Design." *Software Testing & Quality Engineering* 1(1):22–28.

Gilb, Tom. 2005. *Competitive Engineering: A Handbook for Systems Engineering, Requirements Engineering, and Software Engineering Using Planguage*. Oxford, England: Elsevier Butterworth-Heinemann.

Gilb, Tom, and Dorothy Graham. 1993. *Software Inspection*. Reading, MA: Addison-Wesley.

Gottesdiener, Ellen. 2002. *Requirements by Collaboration: Workshops for Defining Needs*. Boston: Addison-Wesley.

_____. 2005. *The Software Requirements Memory Jogger: A Pocket Guide to Help Software and Business Teams Develop and Manage Requirements*. Salem, NH: GOAL/QPC.

Hannah, Jaye. 2022. "What Exactly Is Wireframing? A Comprehensive Guide." https://careerfoundry.com/en/blog/ux-design/what-is-a-wireframe-guide.

Hendrickson, Elisabeth. 2008. "Driving Development with Tests: ATDD and TDD." https://www.stickyminds.com/sites/default/files/presentation/file/2013/08STRWR_T13.pdf.

Hokanson, Candase, and Carlon Halmenschlager Szymanski. 2022. "Got Credit? Using Agile and Visual Models to Roll Out a Global Credit Transformation at Dell." https://www.agilealliance.org/resources/experience-reports/got-credit-using-agile-and-visual-models-to-roll-out-a-global-credit-transformation-at-dell.

IIBA. 2015. *A Guide to the Business Analysis Body of Knowledge (BABOK Guide), 3rd Ed*. Toronto, ON, Canada: International Institute of Business Analysis.

Inflectra. 2020. "Change and Configuration Management of Requirements." https://www.inflectra.com/Ideas/Whitepaper/Change-and-Configuration-Management-of-Requirements.aspx.

ISO/IEC. 2019. *ISO/IEC 25030:2019(en) Systems and software engineering—Systems and software quality requirements and evaluation (SQuaRE)—Quality requirements framework*. https://www.iso.org/obp/ui/#iso:std:iso-iec:25030:ed-2:v1:en.

ISO/IEC/IEEE. 2018. *ISO/IEC/IEEE 29148:2018 Systems and software engineering—Life cycle processes—Requirements engineering*. https://www.iso.org/standard/72089.html.

Kulak, Daryl, and Eamonn Guiney. 2004. *Use Cases: Requirements in Context, 2nd Ed*. Boston: Addison-Wesley.

Kyne, Daniel. 2022. "7 Principles For Writing Great Problem Statements." https://fullstackresearcher.substack.com/p/7-principles-for-writing-great-problem.

Lauesen, Soren. 2002. *Software Requirements: Styles and Techniques*. Boston: Addison-Wesley.

Lawrence, Richard, and Peter Green. 2022. "The Humanizing Work Guide to Splitting User Stories." https://www.humanizingwork.com/the-humanizing-work-guide-to-splitting-user-stories.

Leffingwell, Dean. 2011. *Agile Software Requirements: Lean Requirements Practices for Teams, Programs, and the Enterprise*. Boston: Addison-Wesley.

Li, Shaojun, and Suo Duo. 2014. "Safety analysis of software requirements: model and process." *Procedia Engineering* 80:153–164. https://www.researchgate.net/publication/275540201_Safety_Analysis_of_Software_Requirements_Model_and_Process/fulltext/5552a9ff08ae6fd2d81d5b77/Safety-Analysis-of-Software-Requirements-Model-and-Process.pdf.

Lucidchart. 2022a. "How to draw 5 types of architectural diagrams." https://www.lucidchart.com/blog/how-to-draw-architectural-diagrams.

_____. 2022b. "How to perform a stakeholder analysis." https://www.lucidchart.com/blog/how-to-do-a-stakeholder-analysis.

Malak, Haissam Abdul. 2022. "What is Business Rules Engine: The Complete Guide." https://theecmconsultant.com/business-rules-engine.

McLeod, Saul. 2009. "Short Term Memory." https://www.simplypsychology.org/short-term-memory.html.

McManus, John. 2005. *Managing Stakeholders in Software Development Projects*. Oxford, England: Elsevier Butterworth-Heinemann.

Merriam-Webster Thesaurus. 2022. https://www.merriam-webster.com/thesaurus/elicit.

Miller, Roxanne E. 2009. *The Quest for Software Requirements*. Milwaukee, WI: MavenMark Books, LLC.

Moore, Geoffrey A. 2014. *Crossing the Chasm: Marketing and Selling Disruptive Products to Mainstream Customers, 3rd Ed*. New York: HarperBusiness.

Morgan, Tony. 2002. *Business Rules and Information Systems: Aligning IT with Business Goals*. Boston: Addison-Wesley.

Morris, Latoya. 2022. "Understanding Responsibility Assignment Matrix (RACI Matrix)." https://project-management.com/understanding-responsibility-assignment-matrix-raci-matrix.

Munagavalasa, Chandra. 2014. "Excite and Delight Your Customers by Using the Kano Model." https://www.agileconnection.com/article/excite-and-delight-your-customers-using-kano-model.

Nalimov, Constantine. 2021. "What is a conceptual data model? With examples!" https://www.gleek.io/blog/conceptual-data-model.html.

North, Dan. 2006. "Introducing BDD." https://dannorth.net/introducing-bdd.

Pichler, Roman. 2016. "Use Decision Rules to Make Better Product Decisions." https://www.romanpichler.com/blog/decision-rules-to-make-better-product-decisions.

ProductPlan. 2022. "Minimum Viable Product (MVP)." https://www.productplan.com/glossary/minimum-viable-product.

Robertson, Suzanne, and James Robertson. 2013. *Mastering the Requirements Process: Getting Requirements Right, 3rd Ed*. Boston: Addison-Wesley.

Scaled Agile. 2021a. "Nonfunctional Requirements." https://www.scaledagileframework.com/nonfunctional-requirements.

_____. 2021b. "Weighted Shortest Job First." https://www.scaledagileframework.com/wsjf.

ScienceDirect. 2022. "Physical Data Model." https://www.sciencedirect.com/topics/computer-science/physical-data-model.

Sharma, Lakshay. 2021. "Equivalence Partitioning—A Black Box Testing Technique." https://www.toolsqa.com/software-testing/istqb/equivalence-partitioning.

_____. 2022. "Boundary Value Analysis—A Black Box Testing Technique." https://www.toolsqa.com/software-testing/istqb/boundary-value-analysis.

Simmons, Erik. 2001. "Quantifying Quality Requirements Using Planguage." https://www.geocities.ws/g/i/gillani/SE%272%20Full%20Lectures/ASE%20-%20%20Planguage%20Quantifying%20Quality%20Requirements.pdf.

Simplilearn. 2022. "PMI-ACP Training: Agile Prioritization Techniques." https://www.simplilearn.com/agile-prioritization-techniques-article.

Smith, John. 2023. "13 BEST Requirements Management Tools & Software (2023)." https://www.guru99.com/requirement-management-tools.html.

Sommerville, Ian, and Pete Sawyer. 1997. *Requirements Engineering: A Good Practice Guide*. Chichester, England: John Wiley & Sons, Ltd.

Tableau. 2022. "Root Cause Analysis Explained: Definition, Examples, and Methods." https://www.tableau.com/learn/articles/root-cause-analysis.

Thayer, Richard H., and Merlin Dorfman, eds. 1997. *Software Requirements Engineering, 2nd Ed*. Los Alamitos, CA: IEEE Computer Society Press.

Thomas, Steven. 2008. "Agile Project Planning." https://itsadeliverything.com/agile-project-planning.

Tran, Vu Nguyen, Long Vu Tran, Viet Nguyen Tran, and Dao Ngoc Vu. 2022. "Hazard Analysis Methods for Software Safety Requirements Engineering." ICSIM 2022: 2022 The 5th International Conference on Software Engineering and Information Management (ICSIM), pp. 11–18. https://dl.acm.org/doi/10.1145/3520084.3520087.

von Halle, Barbara. 2002. *Business Rules Applied: Building Better Systems Using the Business Rules Approach*. New York: John Wiley & Sons, Inc.

Weilkiens, Tim. 2007. *Systems Engineering with SysML/UML: Modeling, Analysis, Design*. Burlington, MA: Morgan Kaufmann Publishers.

Wheatcraft, Lou. 2015. "Why Do I Need to Baseline My Requirements?" https://argondigital.com/blog/product-management/why-do-i-need-to-baseline-my-requirements.

Wiegers, Karl E. 2002. *Peer Reviews in Software: A Practical Guide*. Boston: Addison-Wesley.

_____. 2006. *More About Software Requirements: Thorny Issues and Practical Advice*. Redmond, WA: Microsoft Press.

_____. 2007. *Practical Project Initiation: A Handbook with Tools*. Redmond, WA: Microsoft Press.

Wiegers, Karl. n.d. "Why Modeling Is an Essential Business Analysis Technique." https://www.modernanalyst.com/Resources/Articles/tabid/115/ID/5438/Why-Modeling-Is-an-Essential-Business-Analysis-Technique.aspx.

_____. 2019. "Making Peer Reviews Work for You." https://medium.com/analysts-corner/making-peer-reviews-work-for-you-4a63533e0ab6.

_____. 2020a. "It's Only Logical: Decision Tables and Decision Trees." https://medium.com/analysts-corner/its-only-logical-decision-tables-and-decision-trees-12a8b52243ea.

_____. 2020b. "Requirements Review Challenges." https://medium.com/analysts-corner/requirements-review-challenges-e3ffe3ad60ef.

_____. 2022. *Software Development Pearls: Lessons from Fifty Years of Software Experience*. Boston: Addison-Wesley.

Wiegers, Karl, and Joy Beatty. n.d.a. "Agile Requirements: What's the Big Deal?" https://www.modernanalyst.com/Resources/Articles/tabid/115/ID/3573/Agile-Requirements-Whats-the-Big-Deal.aspx.

_____. n.d.b. "Specifying Quality Requirements With Planguage." https://www.modernanalyst.com/Resources/Articles/tabid/115/articleType/ArticleView/articleId/2926/Specifying-Quality-Requirements-With-Planguage.aspx.

_____. 2013. *Software Requirements, 3rd Ed*. Redmond, WA: Microsoft Press.

Wikipedia. 2022. "List of system quality attributes." https://en.wikipedia.org/wiki/List_of_system_quality_attributes.

Withall, Stephen. 2007. *Software Requirement Patterns*. Redmond, WA: Microsoft Press.

Index

Numbers

5 Whys, 15–16

A

abbreviations, defining in glossary, 129
abstraction levels of requirements,
    111–112
acceptance
    criteria, 57, 79, 111–112, 113, 135–136
    tests, 135–136
acronyms, defining in glossary, 127, 129
action enabler, as business rule type, 122
active voice, writing in, 110
activity diagram, 87
agile projects
    baselines on, 143–144, 146
    data interfaces and, 66
    minimum viable product, 104
    nonfunctional requirements on, 71–72
    prioritization on, 98, 101
    product owner, 8, 41
    prototyping on, 92
    requirements management on,
        152–153
    use cases on, 50
    user stories and, 50, 78, 110–111
alternative flow, use case, 48–49
ambiguity, in requirements, 109
analysis, requirements
    activities, 76
    defined, 5–6, 75
    of individual requirements, 77–81
    iteration on, 76

modeling requirements, 84–91
practices for, 76
prioritization of requirements, 83,
    97–105
prototypes, 91–97
of sets of requirements, 81–83
analysis models. *See also* modeling,
    requirements
    activity diagram, 87
    business data diagram, 61
    business objectives model, 22–23
    context diagram, 28–29
    data flow diagram, 63–64, 86
    data models, 60, 61
    decision table, 86, 124–125
    decision tree, 86
    ecosystem map, 29–30
    entity relationship diagram, 61–62, 86
    feature tree, 77–78, 86, 145
    fishbone diagram, 16
    flowchart, 87
    Ishikawa diagram, 16
    objective chain, 23
    process flow, 87–88
    requirements mapping matrix, 87
    root cause analysis diagram, 16
    state-transition diagram, 57–58, 87,
        89–90
    state table, 87
    strawman, 90
    testing, 136–138
analyst, business. *See* business analyst
aphantasia, 85
architecture, 69, 71, 93
assumed requirements, 83

assumptions
    defined, 80
    in requirements analysis, 80
    in use cases, 51
attributes
    quality. *See* quality attributes
    requirement, 113

B

backlog, product
    baselining items in, 143, 146
    management of, 8, 40, 41
    prioritization of, 98
    quality attributes in, 71
baseline, requirements
    agreeing upon, 145–146
    approving, 145–146
    benefits of, 144, 148
    defined, 142–143
    feature tree and, 145
    identifying contents of, 144–145
    managing changes to, 152–153, 155
    managing multiple, 147–148
    models and, 144–145
    scope-bound, 144
    strategies for, 143–144
    time-bound, 143
Beatty, Joy, 22–23
black-box tests, 135, 138–139
Blais, Steven, 21, 36
boundaries, solution, 26–33
    applying, 30–32
    context diagram, 28–29
    ecosystem map, 29–30
    questions to determine, 26–27
    selecting, 27–28
boundary value analysis, 138–139
BPMN (Business Process Model and
        Notation), 85
Brosseau, Jim, 102
business analysis
    professional organizations for, 9
    resources for information, 7–8

business analyst
    requirements elicitation, 45–46
    and requirements review, 132–133
    skills for, 9
    synonyms for, 8
    as team role, 8–9, 35
business data diagram, 61
business events, 54–55
business objectives
    as business requirement type, 4, 19
    defined, 22
    examples of, 22
    modeling, 23
    quantifying, 22
    specifying, 22
    success metrics, 23–24
    use in decision making, 42
    use in determining solution
        boundaries, 31, 32
    use in finding stakeholders, 34
    use in prioritization, 98
    use in requirements analysis, 81, 87
    use in requirements management, 154
business objectives model, 22–23
business opportunities, 14, 17, 19, 20, 24
business problem
    analysis, 13–18
    defined, 14
    template for, 17
Business Process Model and Notation
        (BPMN), 85
business requirements,
    defined, 4, 19
    kinds of information in, 20–21
    questions to explore, 19–20
    vision and scope document for, 20–21,
        116
    vision statement, 24–25
    use in decision making, 42
business rules
    applying, 125–126
    data and, 63, 123
    decision tables and, 124–125
    defined, 4, 121–122

discovering, 123–124
documenting, 124–125
as enterprise-level asset, 11, 123
examples, 121, 124
as origin of functional
    requirements, 80
patterns for writing, 122–123
reusing, 11, 123
sources of, 123–124
types of, 122
use cases and, 51
business rules engine, 126
business systems analyst. *See* business
    analyst

C

cardinality in entity relationship
    diagram, 62
CCB (change or configuration control
    board), 152, 154
change, requirements
    against a baseline, 149
    on agile projects, 149
    anticipating, 10, 150–151
    assessing impact of, 154–155
    communicating decisions, 155
    contingency buffers and, 151
    cost of, 151, 155
    impact assessment, 154–155
    incorporating changes in baseline,
        149–150
    managing, 149, 155
    process for managing, 151–154
    sources of, 150
    status of a change request, 152
change control board (CCB), 152
change control process
    defining, 151–152
    process flow for, 152–154
characteristics
    of good requirements, 79
    of good requirement sets, 82
charter, project, 20–21

Chen, Anthony, 22–23
collaboration in requirements
    engineering, 10
communication in specification
    activities, 10
complexity, managing requirements,
    111–112
computation, as business rule type, 122
concept, solution, 22–23, 27–28, 32
conceptual data model, 60, 61, 86
configuration control board (CCB), 152
conflicts
    between requirements, 76, 82
    across user groups, 36
constraints
    as business rule type, 63, 122
    on data, 60, 63
    defined, 4, 80
    project, 80
    quality attributes and, 69
    solution, 20, 28, 80
    sources of, 41
containers for requirements, 3, 116,
    117–119
context diagram, 28–29, 31, 60, 63, 144
contingency buffers, 151
criteria, acceptance. *See* acceptance
    criteria
criteria matrix for prioritization, 101, 103
crow's foot notation, 62
CRUD (create, read, update, delete)
    operations, 62, 86
customers
    as stakeholders, 36–37
    user classes and, 36–37

D

data
    CRUD functionality, 62
    eliciting requirements for, 59–67
    governance, 60, 66
    output requirements, 63
data dictionary, 64–66

data flow diagram (DFD), 63–64, 86
data models
    business rules in, 63, 123
    conceptual, 60, 61, 86
    glossary entries from, 128
    logical, 60, 86
    physical, 60, 61, 86
data objects
    business rules and, 63, 80, 123
    constraints and, 63
    enabling functionality of, 62
    identifying, 60–61
    modeling, 60–61, 63, 86
    and their relationships, 60–62
data requirements
    business rules as source of, 123
    defined, 4
    eliciting, 59–67
    finding hidden, 66
    quality attributes as source of, 69–70
    specifying, 65
databases, storing requirements in, 3,
        107, 119–120
decision leader, 41–43
decision makers, 39–44, 150, 152
    identifying, 40–41
decision rules, 41–43
decision table, 86
    for business rules, 124–125
    for tests, 136
decision tree, 86, 125
decisions
    classes of requirements-related, 39–40
    communicating, 155
    recording, 43
decomposition, requirements, 77–79
dependencies between
        requirements, 76, 82
deriving requirements from use case,
        48–51, 52, 77–79
DFD, 63–64, 86
diagrams. *See* analysis models
documentation. *See* specification,
        requirements

documents, requirements. *See*
        requirements documents
duplication of requirements, 82

E

ecosystem map, 29–30, 31, 60
elicitation, requirements
    abstraction levels in, 50
    of business requirements, 19–20
    of business rules, 123
    of data requirements, 59–67
    defined, 22, 45
    from events and responses, 53–59
    feature-focused, 47
    participants in, 46
    practices for, 46
    in problem analysis, 15–17
    of quality attributes, 67–73
    techniques for, 46
    usage-centric, 47–53
    use cases and, 49, 51
    of user requirements, 48–51
    user stories and, 50
entities, data, 61
entity relationship diagram (ERD),
        61–62, 86
epic, 50, 51, 78, 112
equivalence partitioning, 138–139
ERD. *See* entity relationship diagram
event analysis, 53–59
event-response table, 56–57
events
    business, 54–55
    classifying, 54, 55
    defined, 54
    examples, 55
    modeling, 56–58
    signal, 54, 55
    specifying, 55–59
    temporal, 54, 55
    testing and, 58–59
    types of, 54–55
evolutionary prototype, 97

exceptions, 79, 81
  use case, 48–49, 52
executable prototype, 94, 96–97
external interface requirements, 4
  data dictionary and, 64–66
  data for, 64–66
  defined, 4
  eliciting, 31

F

fact, as business rule type, 122
feature tree, 77–78, 86, 145
feature-centric elicitation, 47
features, 77–78, 90, 103, 117–118, 145
  abstraction level of, 112
  business objectives and, 22–23
  prioritization of, 101, 103–104
  product, 77–78, 112, 117
  vision statement and, 24
feeding buffers, 151
fidelity of prototype, 93–96
fishbone diagram, 16
fit criteria, 71–72, 134
Five Whys, 15–16
flowchart, 87
flows in a use case
  alternative, 48
  normal, 48
front, pushing quality to the,
    10, 139
functional requirements
  business rules as source,
    125–126
  data models as source, 66
  defined, 4
  deriving from use cases, 48–51,
    52, 77–79
  patterns for writing, 109–111
  practices for eliciting, 46
  quality attributes as source,
    69–70
  testing of, 134

G

gaps in requirements, 6, 81
gathering requirements. *See* elicitation,
    requirements
Gilb, Tom, 114
Given-When-Then pattern, 135–136
glossary
  contents of, 127–129
  data model as source for,
    128–129
  as enterprise-level asset, 127
  project, 127

H

happy path, use case, 48
hazard analysis, 80

I

IDEF0, 85
IIBA (International Institute of Business
    Analysis), 5, 9
IKIWISI acronym, 91–92
impact assessment for requirements
    changes, 154–155
implied requirements, 83
inconsistencies between
    requirements, 82
inference, as business rule type, 122
inspection, as requirement review
    technique, 133
interaction design prototype, 92–94
INVEST acronym, 79
IREB (International Requirements
    Engineering Board), 9
Ishikawa diagram, 16
iterative modeling, 90–91

K

Kano model for prioritization, 101

L

labeling requirements, 82, 113, 119
Lister, Tim, 33
logical data model, 61

M

main flow, use case, 48
main success scenario, use case, 48
management, requirements
        activities, 141–142
    baselining, 142–149
    change management, 149–155
    defined, 5, 141
    practices for, 142
    requirements traceability, 142
    tools, 119–120
managing requirements complexity,
        111–112
Miller, Roxanne, 69
Miller's Magic Number, 84
minimum viable product (MVP), 104
missing requirements, 81, 84, 86, 87, 116,
        125, 134
model simulation prototype, 94
modeling, requirements, 84–91
    benefits of, 84–85
    comparing models, 85–87
    iteration in, 90–91
    languages of, 85
    refining understanding, 87–90
    selecting, 85–87
    strawman models, 90
    testing models, 136–138
    types of models, 3, 85–87
models. *See* analysis models; modeling,
        requirements
MoSCoW prioritization, 100
MVP (minimum viable product), 104

N

navigable wireframe prototype, 94
negotiating requirement priorities, 83
nonfunctional requirements. *See also*
        quality attributes

agile projects and, 71–72
    defined, 4
    specifying with Planguage, 114
    writing, 114
normal flow, use case

O

objective chain model, 23
objectives, business. *See* business
        objectives
objectives for incremental releases, 31
opportunities, business, 14, 17, 19,
        20, 24

P

pairwise comparison for prioritization,
        101, 102–103
passaround review, 133
patterns, writing requirements,
        109–111
peer deskcheck review, 133
peer reviews. *See* reviews, requirements
physical data model, 60, 61
Planguage, 114
PMI (Project Management Institute), 9
postconditions, 51
practices for requirements
        engineering, 5–8
preconditions, 51, 57, 78, 135
prioritization, requirements
    on agile projects, 104
    analytical methods, 103–104
    challenges, 98
    combining methods, 104
    factors that influence, 99
    granularity, 100
    need for, 83
    negotiating, 83
    quality attributes, 70–71, 102–103
    questions to ask, 98
    techniques for, 100–101
priority, as requirement attribute, 113
problem, business. *See* business problem
problem analysis, 13–18

problem statement template, 17
process flow, 87–88, 151–154
process workers, 36
product backlog, 8, 40, 41, 71, 98, 143, 146
product champions, 38
product manager, 8
product owner, 8
   change management and, 147,
      151–152
   as requirements decision leader, 41
product vision. *See* vision statement
professional organizations for business
     analysts, 9
project
   constraints, 80
   defined, 2
   versus product teams, 2
   scope, 24
project buffers, 151
project charter, 20–21
Project Management Institute (PMI), 9
prototypes
   evolutionary, 97
   executable, 94, 96–97
   fate of, 96–97
   fidelity of, 94–95
   interaction design, 92–94
   model simulation, 94
   navigable wireframe, 94
   reasons to create, 91–93
   sketch, 94
   technical design, 92–93
   throwaway, 96
   types of, 94
   wireframe, 94
prototyping
   on agile projects, 92
   reasons to do, 91–93
   tips for, 95–96

Q

qualities
   of good requirement sets, 82
   of good requirements, 79

quality,
   product, 68
   pushing to the front, 10, 139
quality attributes
   architectural implications, 69, 71
   defined, 4, 67
   eliciting, 68–69
   examples of, 68
   external, 68
   fit criteria and, 71–72
   implications of, 69–70
   internal, 68
   as origin of functional
      requirements, 69–70
   prioritizing, 70–71, 102–103
   questions to elicit, 68–69
   reusing, 70
   security, 69–70
   specifying, 71–72, 114
   trade-offs between, 70–71
   types of, 68
quality of service requirements. *See*
     quality attributes
questions requirements let you answer, 1–2
questions to ask
   for change control process, 151–152
   for characterizing stakeholders, 37
   for defining solution boundaries, 26–27
   for eliciting business requirements,
     19–20, 47
   for eliciting data requirements, 59–60
   for eliciting quality attributes, 68–69
   for identifying stakeholders, 34
   for prioritizing requirements, 98

R

RACI matrix, 38
rank ordering for prioritization, 101
relationships between data objects, 60–62
relative weighting for prioritization, 101
release objectives, 31
requirements
   abstraction levels of, 111–112
   analysis. *See* analysis, requirements

assumed, 83
attributes, 113
baseline. *See* baseline, requirements
business. *See* business requirements
change management, 149–155
characteristics of good, 79, 82
classification schema, 3
conflicts between, 82
containers for, 3
data. *See* data requirements
decomposition of, 77–78
defined, 2–3
dependencies between, 82
derived, 5, 63, 69, 78–79, 125, 126, 134
elicitation. *See* elicitation,
    requirements
external interface. *See* external
    interface requirements
functional. *See* functional
    requirements
gaps in, 81
gathering. *See* elicitation,
    requirements
implied, 83
iterative development of, 6, 10
labeling, 82, 113, 119
levels of abstraction of, 111–112
management. *See* management,
    requirements
missing, 81, 84, 86, 87, 116, 125, 134
modeling. *See* modeling, requirements
nonfunctional. *See* nonfunctional
    requirements
origin of, 26, 77
prioritization. *See* prioritization,
    requirements
quality. *See* quality attributes
questions answered by, 1–2
rationale for, 77, 113
reusing, 11, 80–81. *See also* reuse
reviewing, 132–134
risks from, 80
solution. *See* solution requirements
specification. *See* specification,
    requirements

status, 113
system, 4
terminology, 2
traceability, 82, 87, 120, 142
types of, 4–5
user. *See* user requirements
validation. *See* validation,
    requirements
version control, 113, 141
writing. *See* writing requirements
requirements analysis. *See* analysis,
    requirements
requirements analyst. *See* business analyst
requirements development
    as incremental and iterative
        activity, 6, 10
    subdomains of, 5–6
requirements documents, 3, 20–21, 116–119
requirements elicitation. *See* elicitation,
    requirements
requirements engineer. *See* business analyst
requirements engineering
    collaboration in, 10
    good practices for, 5–8
    resources for information, 7–8
requirements management. *See*
    management, requirements
requirements mapping matrix (RMM), 87
Requirements Modeling Language
    (RML), 22–23, 85
requirements specification. *See*
    specification, requirements
requirements traceability matrix, 142
requirements validation. *See* validation,
    requirements
reuse
    of business rules, 123
    of ecosystem map, 30
    of glossary, 127
    of quality attributes, 70
    of requirements, 11, 80–81
    of stakeholder catalog, 37
reviews, requirements, 132–134
    participants, 132–133
    types of, 133

risk
    from requirements, 80
    thinking, 10
RML (Requirements Modeling
        Language), 22–23, 85
RMM (requirements mapping matrix), 87
Robertson, James, 71, 134
Robertson, Suzanne, 71, 134
root cause analysis, 14–17
    diagram, 16
rules, business. *See* business rules
rules, decision, 41–43

S

Sawyer, Pete, 2
Scaled Agile Framework, 71–72
scenarios, use cases and, 48–51
Schmidt, Eugenia, 75
scope, 24, 28, 31, 32, 40, 143–145
    depicting with a feature tree, 145
scope-bound baseline, 144
security requirements, 69–70
sets of requirements, analyzing, 81–83
shall, as requirements keyword, 109–111
signal events, 54, 55
signing off, 132, 146
sketch prototype, 94
Software Requirement Patterns
        (Withall), 65
software requirements specification (SRS)
    as container, 117–119
    template for, 117
solution
    acceptance criteria for, 135–136
    analyzing a proposed, 15–17, 18
    business objectives and, 22–23
    concept, 23, 27–28
    constraints, 80
    defined, 2
    eliciting business requirements for, 20
    ideas, 80, 104
    incremental delivery of, 147–148
    prototyping, 91–97

requirements. *See* solution
        requirements
    understanding what users need to do
        with, 47–53
    vision of, 24
solution boundaries, 26–33
    applying, 30–32
    context diagram, 28–29
    ecosystem map, 29–30
    questions to define, 26–27
solution requirements, 4, 67, 116, 117
Somerville, Ian, 2
Speak-Out.biz
    acceptance tests for, 136
    stakeholder profile for, 37–38
    use cases for, 49
    user classes for, 36–37
specification, requirements. *See also*
        software requirements
        specification; writing requirements
    communication in, 10
    content of, 107
    defined, 6, 107
    detail in, 108
    form of, 108
    formality of, 108
    practices for, 108
    structure of, 107–108, 115–121
SRS. *See* software requirements
        specification
stack ranking for prioritization, 101
stakeholders, 33–39. *See also* decision
        makers
    catalog, 34, 38
    characterizing, 37–38
    classes of, 35
    customers and, 36–37
    defined, 33
    identifying, 33–34
    overlooked, 33
    profile, 37–38
    questions to ask when looking for, 34
    representatives of, 33, 38
    template for profiling, 37–38
    user classes and, 36–37

state table, 87

statechart diagram. *See* state-transition diagram

state-transition diagram, 57–58, 87, 89–90

status
  for change requests, 152
  of data objects, 87, 89
  of requirements, 113, 141

strawman models, 90

structured analysis, 85

subdomains, requirements development, 5–6

success metrics, 23–24

synonyms, defining in glossary, 127, 129

system boundary, 28–29

system events. *See* events

system requirements, 4, 107

system requirements specification, 3, 108, 118, 133

systems analyst. *See* business analyst

Systems Modeling Language (SysML), 85

T

team review, 133

technical debt, 96–97

technical design prototype, 92–93

templates, 115–117
  acceptance tests, 135
  benefits of, 116–117
  problem statement, 17
  project charter, 21
  software requirements specification, 117
  stakeholder profile, 37–38
  tailoring, 116–117
  use case, 51
  user story, 50, 110
  vision and scope document, 20–21
  vision statement, 24–25

temporal events, 54, 55

terminology, requirements, 2

terms
  as business rule type, 122
  defining in glossary, 127–130

testing
  acceptance, 135–136
  analysis models, 136–138
  black-box, 135, 138–139
  boundary value analysis, 138–139
  equivalence partitioning, 138–139
  events and, 58–59
  Given-When-Then, 135–136
  pushing quality to the front, 139
  requirements, 134–139
  use cases and, 52
  user stories and, 136

three-level scale for prioritization, 100

throwaway prototype, 96

time-bound baseline, 143

traceability, requirements, 82, 87, 120, 142

trigger, use case, 51

U

UML (Unified Modeling Language), 85

usage-centric requirements elicitation, 47–53

use cases
  agile projects and, 50
  business rules and, 51
  deriving functional requirements from, 48–51, 52, 77–79
  deriving tests from, 134
  exceptions, 48–49, 79
  flows, 48–49
  naming convention for, 49
  postconditions, 51
  preconditions, 51, 78
  prioritization and, 52
  scenarios and, 48–51
  template for, 51
  testing and, 52

user classes
  direct and indirect, 36
  examples of, 36–37
  favored, 36, 41, 99
  product champions and, 38
  as stakeholders, 36–37

user representatives, 38
user requirements, 5. *See also* use cases;
    user stories
  applying, 52
  defined, 5
  eliciting, 47–53
user stories, 50–51
  epics and, 50, 78, 112
  prioritization and, 52
  testing and, 52
  use cases and, 50–51
  writing requirements, 110–111
users. *See also* stakeholders
  direct and indirect, 36
  product champions as
    representatives, 38

V

validation, requirements
  defined, 6, 131–132
  practices for, 132
  prototypes and, 92, 93, 94
  requirements reviews. *See* reviews,
    requirements
  testing requirements, 134–139
  versus verification, 131
version control, requirements, 113, 141

vision and scope document, 20–21, 37,
    48, 118
  as container for business requirements,
    3, 20, 26
  template for, 21
vision statement, template
  for, 24–25
visual models. *See* analysis models
voice of the customer, 38

W

website for this book, 6
Weighted Shortest Job First (WSJF)
    prioritization method, 101
why, asking, 15–16
wireframe prototype, 94
Withall, Stephen, 65
writing requirements, 109–115
  abstraction levels of, 111–112
  good practices for, 110
  nonfunctional requirements, 114
  patterns for, 109–111
  as representing requirements
    knowledge, 109
  requirement attributes, 113
WSJF (Weighted Shortest Job First)
    prioritization method, 101

Register Your Product at informit.com/register

Access additional benefits and save up to 65%* on your next purchase

- Automatically receive a coupon for 35% off books, eBooks, and web editions and 65% off video courses, valid for 30 days. Look for your code in your InformIT cart or the Manage Codes section of your account page.

- Download available product updates.

- Access bonus material if available.**

- Check the box to hear from us and receive exclusive offers on new editions and related products.

InformIT—The Trusted Technology Learning Source

InformIT is the online home of information technology brands at Pearson, the world's leading learning company. At informit.com, you can

- Shop our books, eBooks, and video training. Most eBooks are DRM-Free and include PDF and EPUB files.

- Take advantage of our special offers and promotions (informit.com/promotions).

- Sign up for special offers and content newsletter (informit.com/newsletters).

- Access thousands of free chapters and video lessons.

- Enjoy free ground shipping on U.S. orders.*

* Offers subject to change.

** Registration benefits vary by product. Benefits will be listed on your account page under Registered Products.

Connect with InformIT—Visit informit.com/community

 twitter.com/informit

 Pearson

informIT·

Addison-Wesley • Adobe Press • Cisco Press • Microsoft Press • Oracle Press • Peachpit Press • Pearson IT Certification • Que